Presented to

_____

From

_____

Internal Affairs

Emotional Stability
In an Unstable World

By Dr. Larry J. Hutton

Internal Affairs
© 2004 by Dr. Larry J. Hutton
P. O. Box 822
Broken Arrow, OK 74013-0822

Published by Force of Faith Publications
P.O. Box 822
Broken Arrow, OK 74013-0822
ISBN: 0-9747558-0-X

Original Cover Art:
    David Wirginis
Interior Design:
    Larry Hutton
Editors:
    Stephen Rankin
    Jennifer Sutton
    Andrea Spear
    Larry Hutton

Contents

Acknowledgements

Thanks to my right-hand man, Steve Rankin, for your commitment and dedication to LARRY HUTTON MINISTRIES, and especially for your passionate effort in the preparation of this manuscript.

Thanks to my wonderful staff at LHM for all the "work of the ministry" you accomplish, enabling me to give myself to the Word and prayer. As a result of us laboring together we can publish books and touch the body of Christ world-wide.

A special and loving thanks to Liz, my wonderful wife since July 1981, for faithfully walking by my side, and for your love, support and understanding as I spent many hours in my office with the composition of this book.

And finally, a special and affectionate thanks to Rachel, my talented and radiant daughter, for your happy and joyful countenance. Your constant laughter, singing and smiling face bring such pleasure and joy to our household.

Dedication

I dedicate this book to my Wife and Queen, Liz, and to my Daughter and Princess, Rachel.

As a Husband and Father, I could not be more fulfilled and proud of my wife and daughter for their dedication to God and to His Kingdom. Their unswerving commitment to travel with me in the ministry has helped me remain focused and strong.

Proverbs 18:22 says that whoever finds a wife finds a good thing and obtains the favor of God. Boy—did I ever find a treasure! When I found Liz it was easy for me to "leave" and "cleave." I am one blessed and highly favored man!

Psalm 127:3 tells me that Rachel is a gift and a reward from the Lord. God must have thought I deserved an extra special reward when he gave me Rachel. I am truly a happy man!

Introduction

Back in 1977 the Lord spoke something to me that was truly amazing and changed my life forever! He told me that He was going to teach me how to live my life in a way that would allow me to maintain total control of my emotions, no matter what was going on in my life. He said that if I would do what He was going to teach me, then I would have no more "down" days, stress-filled days, strife-filled days, or any days filled with hurt feelings, depression, discouragement or uncontrolled anger. He told me that all of those kinds of days would be things of the past—if I would only obey.

My initial thoughts were just as human as yours are. I thought, "That sounds too good to be true! Is it really possible to never have another down day in my life?"

After the Lord spoke those things to me, He began showing me in His Word how to live that kind of lifestyle. Of course, it didn't take a rocket scientist to figure out that it would be wonderful to live that way. So, I began doing what the Lord revealed to me. And it was truly amazing—the Lord knew exactly what He was talking about!

For the next twelve months I did not have one down day, stress-filled day, get-my-feelings-hurt day, or any of the other things He had mentioned. It was heaven on earth! As you can imagine, after living that way for one whole year I didn't want to stop! So I continued the next year, and the next year, and the next year and…

Now, after all these years, I can truly say I have not had a down day since 1977. No days of hurt feelings (you know, where you wear your feelings on your shirt sleeve), no days of uncontrolled anger, no depressed days, no discouraged days, no stress-filled days and no strife-filled days. Now don't take me wrong—I HAVE PASSED UP A LOT OF MARVELOUS OPPORTUNITES TO HAVE ALL OF THOSE KINDS OF DAYS! But the key is that I *passed them up*!

Of course, when people hear that kind of wonderful

news, they want to know how I did it. So, I felt in my heart that the Lord wanted me to share with others how to live this kind of lifestyle.

In the world today there are many pressures coming at us from all directions. These pressures can cause us to live on an emotional roller coaster. However, God has designed a way whereby His children can live their lives with their emotions under complete control—at all times and under all circumstances!

This book shares many of the things that God revealed to me back in 1977, as well as many other precious truths that have been revealed since that time. My prayer for you is that you will be strengthened and encouraged as you read this book, that you will have the eyes of your understanding opened, and that you will take the truths that I share and apply them to your life.

When you are finished reading this book, you will be equipped to live a carefree, worry-free, stress-free and strife-free life!

Happy reading—and may today be the start of a bright and happy future!

CHAPTER

The Sin of Worry

In our society today, worry is running rampant. People are worried about their health, worried about their children, worried about their finances, worried about their jobs, worried about their husbands or wives, worried about getting old, worried about terrorists, worried about what people are thinking about them, and even worried about what someone else is worried about!

Worry is really an offspring of fear,
and fear will paralyze our faith!

Here's the difference between fear and faith. Faith is a reaction from the heart based on something God has said, whereas fear (or worry) is a reaction from the mind or emotions based on something your circumstance (or the devil) has said.

I looked up the word *worry* in Merriam-Webster's Online Dictionary. Used as a noun it means: *"mental distress or agitation resulting from concern usually for something impending or anticipated."* Used as a verb it means: *"...to afflict with mental distress or agitation..."* Notice the words *mental distress.* What does that mean? It means that your mind and emotions are suffering. Look at the following synonyms for the word worry: *agonize, fret, be anxious, be concerned, be troubled, be bothered, be apprehensive, be nervous, be fearful and lose sleep. Stress* is even a form of worry. It has been defined as: *constant worry, pressure, anxiety and nervous tension.* All of these negative forces work in the mental and emotional realm and can be very destructive to many areas of our lives.

Think about how worry operates. The only way we can worry is if we allow our thoughts to be negative ones. Worrisome thoughts never bring us peace or joy.

Let me ask you a question. When we anticipate that something good is about to occur, what happens?

Does it cause us to have a positive outlook and a happy demeanor? Of course! If we think that something wonderful is going to happen, then our countenance brightens and we act like we're glad. On the contrary, when we worry, it means that we are actually afraid that something bad has happened or is going to happen. Worry never deals with the *known* realm—it always deals with the *unknown* realm. People worry about things that they don't know about. When we don't *know* about something, you might say that we are "in the dark." Well—get a grip on this next statement!

Worry never did produce anything in its darkroom except a bunch of negatives.

Worry never dwells on the positive—it always dwells on the negative. "What has happened," "What is going to happen," "What did they think," "How am I going to make it," "What if they don't like me," "What if I blow it," "I don't think I can handle it," etc., are all expressions of worry.

An interesting observation of statements made by those who worry is the fact that most of the time the worry centers on "I" or "me." That means people who worry are more self-conscious than God-conscious. They are being selfish or carnally minded instead of spiritually minded. God said in Romans 8:6 that to be spiritually minded causes us to walk in His life and His peace. Well, when we worry about something, we are not walking in God's peace; therefore we are being carnally minded.

Now someone might say, "Well, I'm not really worried about it, I'm just concerned." If that is what you think, I encourage you to look up the definition of the word *concern*. You'll probably find some or all of these listed: *worried, anxious, troubled, afraid, disturbed, alarmed, fretful, apprehensive, uneasy, nervous or upset.* The bottom line is this: if we are worried about something then we are in fear, not faith. And Romans 14:23b says, *"...whatsoever is not of faith is sin."* The New Jerusalem Bible says it this way, *"...and every action which does not spring from faith is sin."* So that means that the very act of worry is sin!

Look at Philippians 4:6. It starts out saying, *"Be careful for nothing..."* After looking at different Greek concordances you might say it this way, *"Don't be troubled with cares about anything."* By combining different translations of this verse you could say, *"Don't worry, fret or be anxious about anything."*

Listen, the Bible tells us not to worry just as plainly as it tells us not to commit adultery. And yet too many Christians are treating worry like it is a normal part of life. No, No, No—it is not normal to worry—it is abnormal! It is just as wrong for us to worry as it is for us to be involved in adultery, murder or thievery. Are those actions part of a normal person's life? No! And the sad part is that worry appears to be causing more destruction in people's lives than the other three things I just mentioned combined!

Now here's something else to ponder—you cannot worry and be humble at the same time! Worry is a behavior rooted in pride. Let me show you what I'm talking about. Look at 1st Peter, Chapter Five. "Oh, Brother Larry, I know what that says. It tells us to cast our care on the Lord because He cares for us." Yes, verse 7 does tell us that, but the verse starts with the word *"casting."* You don't start a sentence with the word casting. Verse 7 is a continuation of what God was saying in verse 6. Let's look at both verses together.

> **Humble yourselves therefore under the mighty hand of God, that he may exalt you in due time: 7Casting all your care upon him; for he cares for you.**

Notice it tells us to cast ALL our care. If we cast all our care then we would be carefree. *Carefree* has been defined as: *untroubled, lighthearted, relaxed, cheerful or free from care.* Well then, God is telling us right here that He wants us to live a carefree life! But, notice that in verse 6 He starts out by saying, *"Humble yourselves."* And then He tells us that in order to humble ourselves we must cast our cares upon Him. The indication here is that living carefree while walking with God is a true sign of humility. That means the opposite would also be true—living your life in constant worry is a sign that you are operating in pride.

Think about this: God has told us to cast ALL our cares on Him. So if we choose to worry about something, then in essence we are telling God, "Lord, I don't believe that you will take care of this for me, so I will handle this on my own." That places us on the throne of our lives—not God. That, my friend, is pride. And pride will get us into trouble. Proverbs 16:18 says, *"Pride goes before destruction."* Proverbs 29:23 says, *"A man's pride shall bring him low."*

When we worry, pride starts working against us to destroy us and bring us low, or in other words, to cast us down into the muck and mire of depression, discouragement, etc. But God doesn't want us brought low. That's why, in 1st Peter, He tells us to humble ourselves by casting our cares. Notice what verse 6 says that He will do if we humble ourselves. It says that He will *"exalt"* us. The Greek word for *exalt* means *to elevate or lift up*. What do we need elevated or lifted up out of? Evidently, according to the next verse, it is the cares and worries of life. They must be weighing us down, holding us back, causing us to sink and trying to bring us so low that we feel hopeless and want to just give up.

Listen, we were not designed by God to handle the pressures and cares that tomorrow and the next day will bring. God wants to elevate us or lift us up out of every situation that attempts to hold us down. But we must cast our concerns, worries, frustrations and cares upon the Lord so that He can exalt us. When we cast our cares, that act of humility is also an act of faith. We have faith that God is bigger than the situation that we are tempted to worry about and that He will take care of it for us.

Notice again that verses 6 and 7 tell us to humble ourselves under the mighty hand of God by casting our cares upon Him. Notice the phrase *"the mighty hand of God."* That means that God can "hand-le" anything and everything that comes our way. So when we are tempted to worry, let's remember that God is a mighty God and will use His mighty hand to take care of our problems—if we let Him.

Let's look at these two verses again, and then think about what will happen if we do just the opposite of what they tell us to do.

If casting our care will cause us to humble ourselves and allow God's mighty hand to lift us up out of the troubles of life, then worrying about something will cause us to enter into pride and thereby stop God's mighty hand from lifting us up out of those same difficulties.

Let's face it—worry is pride and it's also sin. And sin is not going to make our situations or circumstances change for the better.

Worry does not empty tomorrow's problems,
it just empties today's strength.

Did you get that? Worrying about something today is not going to eliminate the problems that will come tomorrow. But it will empty you of the energy, strength and faith that you need to overcome the troubles that you face today! That being the case, then it will greatly benefit all of us if we will learn how to cast our cares on the Lord.

Now look again at verse 7. It tells us to cast our *"care."* The word *care* comes from the Greek word **merimna,** which means *care and anxiety*. To further our understanding of this word, let's look at two other Scriptures that use the same Greek word.

First of all let's look at Mark 4. It contains the parable of the sower who sows the Word. This parable reveals to us the different conditions of the heart that will cause us to either receive the harvest from the seed or miss out altogether. The verses that we want to look at are verses 18 and 19. These talk about those who allow their hearts to become the type of ground that have thorns growing up out of it.

> **And these are they which are sown among thorns; such as hear the word, [19]And the cares of this world, and the deceitfulness of riches, and the lusts of other things entering in, choke the word, and it becomes unfruitful.**

It says that after they hear the Word, they allow different things to enter into their hearts, which put a stranglehold on the Word. This in turn causes the Word to suffocate so that it can no longer produce any fruit in their lives; thus they miss out on their harvest.

Now, look at the three things that are mentioned that

will choke the Word out of our lives if we allow them to:

1. The cares of this world.
2. The deceitfulness of riches.
3. The lusts of other things.

To remain focused on the purpose of this book, we will just look at the first thing that is listed. It is *"the cares of this world."* The cares of this world will choke the Word out of us, so that it will become unfruitful in our lives. Remember, this word *cares* is the same Greek word used in 1st Peter 5:7. Tying that passage and this passage together, we can see that when we allow ourselves to worry about things that are going on around us (and in the world) we allow the Word to be choked out of us. In essence, we take God out of the picture. We are allowing the problems, rather than His Word, to dictate how we act. This causes us to enter into pride. Then, because we are not acting upon His Word, God is not in a position to lift us up out of our problems.

God does not watch over our problems to get rid of them,
He watches over His Word to accomplish it!
(See Jeremiah 1:12.)

When we believe God's Word and act like it is true,

right in the midst of contradictory circumstances, then God is able to use His mighty hand and change our circumstances. Therefore, we must be aware that, according to this 19th verse in Mark 4, the cares of this world are out to steal the Word from our hearts so that we won't have God working on our behalf.

Okay, we've looked at one of the two Scriptures which used the same Greek word as 1st Peter 5:7. Now let's take a look at the second Scripture that uses the same word. It is found in Luke 21:34.

> **And take heed to yourselves, lest at any time your hearts be overcharged with surfeiting, and drunkenness, and cares of this life, and so that day come upon you unawares.**

The verse starts out by virtually saying, "Be on your guard and watch out!" It sounds like God is trying to warn us, doesn't it? That means we can avoid whatever it is He is warning us about.

He continues His warning by saying, if you are not on your guard you can allow your hearts to become *"overcharged."* The word *overcharged* comes from a Greek word that means *to weigh down*. In other words, you feel depressed, stressed, uptight, or you feel like a bundle of nerves. (Sounds like the same symptoms as worry, doesn't it?)

Then He tells us the three things that we are supposed to guard against that will weigh us down. He lists *surfeiting, drunkenness* and *cares of this life*. The Greek word for *surfeiting* in essence means *the giddiness caused by drinking too much alcohol and the headache that comes as a result of it*. The word *drunkenness* simply means *the condition of being intoxicated*. And the word *cares* is the same word used in 1st Peter 5:7 which means *worry or anxiety*.

The *"cares of this life"* refers to all the things that pop up in our daily lives, such as decisions we have to make, appointments we have to keep, bills we have to pay, automobile problems, mistakes we make, failures that occur, and other unexpected things that catch us off guard—the list goes on and on. God said that the *"cares of this life"* would weigh us down if we allow them to.

That goes right along with what we have already seen both in 1st Peter and in the parable of the sower. The cares and worries will choke the Word out of us and bring us down into the muck and mire of life. Feelings of hopelessness and despair will begin dominating our lives. We will feel like we just can't go on, we just can't make it and we might as well give up. That is what this verse is talking about when it says your heart becomes overcharged.

In addition, this verse of Scripture shows us that there is something else we need to be aware of. The verse says that if your hearts become overcharged with these things then, *"that day will come upon you unawares."* This is saying that we won't be able to discern the times and the seasons, if the cares of life are weighing us down. In essence, it is saying that we won't be able to hear the voice of the Spirit or be spiritually perceptive concerning the things of God.

Listen, God categorizes the worries and anxieties of life right along with surfeiting and drunkenness. That's because people who are in those conditions are not alert, perceptive or sharp, nor do they make intelligent choices concerning themselves or the lives of others. And that's exactly the same category that God puts us in when we worry, get our feelings hurt and fret over every little thing that comes along.

Let me make it very plain—if you allow yourself to continually worry, you are no better off than a drunk!

"Ouch! Brother Larry, that hurt!"

Listen, if we will learn to accept instruction from God's Word, even when it seems to hurt, then God will make sure we get a harvest of righteousness and peace (see Hebrews 12:11). God is trying to make things a whole lot easier for us. You see, when we do things His way we stay yoked up to Jesus. (His yoke is EASY and His burden is LIGHT! Matthew 11:30.)

So, God warns us here in Luke 21:34 that the cares of this life are going to try to move us into worry. And if we enter into worry, the result will be a heart that is overcharged. In other words, we will feel like an emotional wreck, or we will feel stressed out and sometimes even feel like walking away from it all. That puts us in a position where the Word has been choked out of us and has not been allowed to produce any fruit. It also positions us where we will not be spiritually perceptive to the voice of God nor His guidance. And that is a dangerous position to be in.

These prideful and sinful *feelings* can only control us when we are disobeying what God has told us to do. Remember, He told us to *"cast all our cares upon Him."* Then, here in Luke, He told us to *"take heed."* Since God told us to be on our guard and to watch out for the *cares of life,* then we don't have to let them overcome us.

God tells us in Philippians 4:6, *"Be careful for nothing."* The Greek word for *careful* means *to be troubled with cares.* So, He's saying don't be worried, get uptight or be stressed out about anything. In other words, live carefree! John 14:27 says, *"Let not your heart be troubled..."* The Greek word for *troubled* is defined as follows: *to cause one inward commotion; to take away his calmness of mind.* And that is exactly what worry does—it causes inward turmoil and robs you of your peace of mind.

Now listen, God said here in John's gospel, *"Let not your heart be troubled."* That means we have to make a choice. The implication here is that we can *let* things bother us or we can *not let* things bother us—the choice is ours. But God told us to *"not let"* things upset us or bother us and rob us of living a relaxed, peaceful and happy life. If we will obey Him by humbling ourselves and choosing to cast ALL our cares on Him, then He will be our ALL-SUFFICIENT ONE and we will live the abundant life that He created us to live.

CHAPTER

One Thing is Needful

Let's examine a Bible story that illustrates what we have been looking at so far. It can give us further insight regarding what God has to say about worry. The story is found in Luke 10:38-42.

> **Now it came to pass, as they went, that he entered into a certain village: and a certain woman named Martha received him into her house. ³⁹And she had a sister called Mary, which also sat at Jesus' feet, and heard his word.**

> **40But Martha was cumbered about much serving, and came to him, and said, Lord, do you not care that my sister has left me to serve alone? Bid her therefore that she help me. 41And Jesus answered and said unto her, Martha, Martha, you are careful and troubled about many things: 42But one thing is needful: and Mary has chosen that good part, which shall not be taken away from her.**

As the story opens we find Jesus being received into the home of Martha. Her sister Mary, whether living there or just visiting, was also in the home. Mary was sitting on the floor just listening to Jesus share what God had to say. But it says in verse 40 that Martha was *"cumbered."* The Enhanced Strong's Lexicon defines *cumbered* as follows: *"to draw away; distract; to be driven about mentally."* What was it that she was being drawn away from and distracted from? What was it that was causing her to be driven about mentally and emotionally? Let's go on reading and see.

In verse 41 Jesus told Martha that she was *"careful"* and *"troubled."* The word *careful* used here is the same Greek word found in Philippians 4:6 where it tells us to *"be careful for nothing"* or not to worry about anything. The Greek word for *troubled* means *to be disturbed, disquieted or troubled in mind*. So, Jesus told Martha that she was worrying and allowing troubling thoughts in her mind about many things, and that this was causing her to be drawn away from something.

Notice, Jesus did not tell Martha that it was wrong to serve Him. Of course He knew that when you are a guest in someone's home, they are going to do everything possible to make you feel welcomed and comfortable. But that wasn't the issue here. The issue was that Martha was bothered in her mind and was worrying.

Maybe she had gotten busy fixing a meal for Jesus and realized that while she was trying to finish cooking the fish the beans were getting cold. Then while she was reheating the beans and watching the fish—the bread burned. After that she began to worry, allowing thoughts of self to enter in, and without realizing it she opened the door to pride.

Maybe her thoughts turned to "what is Jesus going to think about my cooking?" Then she allowed frustration to enter in and started entertaining thoughts of blaming others. "If that dumb sister of mine would get off her rear end and help me this wouldn't be happening!" Her worry and frustration opened the door to strife. Then, with her emotions out of control, she went to Jesus and complained about the situation. (Note: People who worry usually find something to complain about.)

When Jesus responded to Martha, He didn't even address that particular incident—He went right to the heart of the problem. In essence He said, "Martha, if you weren't worried and troubled in your mind about this situation you would be worried and bothered about something else." In other words, He was telling her that the thing she thought was the problem wasn't the problem at all! The situation became *her* problem because of the way she handled it in her mind. She allowed wrong thinking to dominate her.

So, after Jesus addressed the problem, after He told Martha that she (not other people) was the cause of her problems, He proceeded to help her. He went on to tell Martha how to get out of that type of emotionally draining lifestyle. Look at verses 41-42. In essence, He said, *"Martha, you are losing sleep and allowing yourself to be bothered continuously. But there is one thing that you can do that will deliver you from the emotional disturbances and anxiety you are living in."*

Notice, Jesus said that there was just *one* thing that she needed to do.

At this point Martha may have settled down enough to listen to Jesus. Maybe she was thinking, "Okay, I know I shouldn't have let that bother me. I know I tend to let things get me down, uptight, worried or whatever—so what can I do Jesus? What is the one thing that will help me get free from living on an emotional rollercoaster?"

Now the next thing that Jesus said to Martha is very interesting. He didn't just come out and plainly tell her what she should do. In essence He said, *"Martha, that one thing, the part that you are missing that will make your life good—is what your sister Mary has chosen, and because of her actions it will never be taken away from her."*

Jesus used someone else's life as an example of how to stay free from worry and emotional instability. He used an illustration. When an illustration is added to one's teaching, it's comparable to adding a window to a house—it lets more light in. So Jesus used Mary's life to illustrate to Martha what she needed to do. Why didn't Jesus just come out and plainly tell Martha what to do? Could it be that the Word of God tells us to *"seek and you shall find?"* Maybe Jesus was trying to tell Martha (and us) that quick fixes don't work—we have to dig to find the gem. But *the find is always worth the time.*

Too many Christians want everything handed to them on a silver platter. They run to the healing evangelist hoping that he will lay hands on them and heal them with no responsibility on their part. They run to the prosperity preacher hoping that he will pray for them so that they can prosper regardless of the way they live. They run to the pastor in their emotional upheavals, not wanting the pastor to give them the Word and tell them that they have to act on it, but rather to have him lay hands on them or offer up a prayer that will quickly fix everything. But that is not the way God's system works.

Another thing that many Christians do is try to blame their actions on someone or some thing. But I want us to notice two things that Jesus *did not* say to Martha.

He did not say, "Martha, it is okay that you are feeling this way. I understand that you may be going through some difficult situations right now." In other words, Jesus did not sympathize with Martha even though she may have been facing some challenges in her life.

The other thing that He didn't do was to plainly tell Martha what the one thing was that she needed to do. Since He used Mary's lifestyle as an example, Martha had to assume the responsibility of watching Mary, diligently observing what she did and how she faced life's challenges. What was it that kept Mary from worrying about many things? Whatever she was doing at the moment that Jesus was telling Martha about it, must have been what Mary did at other times as well. Why? Because Jesus had just said that Martha was worried about *"many"* things, and that Mary had chosen something else that kept her free from worrying and getting bothered about many things.

There is a key word that Jesus used here when referring to what Mary did. Notice, He said Mary had *"chosen."* This indicates that Mary had choices to make. In fact, one of the definitions of the Greek word used here means *choosing one out of many.* Mary must have chosen this one thing, instead of the many things she could have chosen, in response to the cares of this life. So, whatever Mary was doing in this particular story must have been what she did on a continual basis, and that was Martha's answer to getting free from worry.

Let's now look at what Mary did.

Verse 39 tells us that Mary *"sat at Jesus' feet and heard the Word."* This shows us that she made a choice to submit to Jesus as her Lord. She was not going to allow life's problems to rule her emotions. She chose to submit to the yoke of Jesus instead. (Remember, His yoke is easy! See Matthew 11:30.) By choosing to submit to Jesus, she placed herself in a position where she *"heard"* the Word. The Greek word for *heard* means: *to hear, to attend to, to consider what is or has been said, to understand.*

Let's use those definitions and apply them to what Mary was doing. Mary was *attending to* the Word. She was *considering what she was hearing* right then, *as well as things that she had already heard.* And she was applying herself *to understand* what was being said. Jesus called the thing that Mary chose the *"good part"* (verse 42). Well, God's Word is called the good Word both in Jeremiah 29:10 and Hebrews 6:5. The good part that Mary had chosen to dwell on and act upon was God's Word. Instead of choosing to worry and be troubled in her mind about many things, she chose to believe and act upon the words of Jesus.

With that understanding we can now see what it was that Jesus told Martha she was *"cumbered"* about. Remember, cumbered means *to be drawn away, distracted, or driven about mentally.* So, I'll ask the question again; what was Martha being drawn away from and distracted from? The Word! Jesus and the Word are one. She was being separated from the Word because she was worrying. Dwelling on wrong thoughts and allowing herself to worry placed her on an emotional rollercoaster. She was being driven about mentally by her cares.

Now allow me to refer to something we learned earlier in this book. First Peter 5:7 tells us to cast our care. Remember, the same Greek word for *care* is also found in the parable of the sower where it says *"the cares of this world,"* and in Luke 21:34 where it talks about our hearts being overcharged with *"cares of this life."* The Greek word means *anxiety and worry.* But it comes from the Greek word **merizo** that means *to be divided, separated into parts, or cut into pieces.* This Greek word is used in Mark 3:24-26 where Jesus says that a kingdom that is *divided* or a house that is *divided* will be unable to stand. This division causes the kingdom or person *to be separated into parts and cut into pieces.*

That's exactly what worry will do to us! It will cause us to be separated into parts or cut into pieces. Worry will divide us from God and His Word. If we are separated from God and His Word then we are no longer walking in the light. If we are separated from the light then we are walking in darkness. That place of darkness is where the Word becomes unfruitful and our hearts become overcharged with stress. That is when frustration, anxiety, fear, depression, or mental and emotional disturbances run rampant. This in turn opens the door for numerous pains and physical problems to operate in our bodies.

This may explain why many doctors who have seen patients with all kinds of physical problems were unable to diagnose the cause. And on occasions they even gave a wrong diagnosis. Very often the patients got frustrated with the doctors because of their inability to identify the problems and their causes.

The pains and illnesses were very real, causing the person much grief in their body, which only added to the emotional and mental problems, thus pushing them further down into misery and unhappiness. Without knowing it, they had allowed themselves to dwell on their problems, thus opening the door for pride. Then the Lord could not lift them up because they were not humbling themselves by casting their cares upon Him.

Furthermore, this place of separation from the Word doesn't affect just the one person. Sooner or later it divides them from their spouse, children, families, friends, jobs, etc. And, unless the person is taught the Word, they will act just like Martha did, and continually pass the blame off on others.

"Oh, Brother Larry, you've hit the nail right on the head! That's exactly what my life is like. I feel like I'm at the end of my rope. I just can't take it anymore. I've tried casting my cares upon the Lord but it just doesn't seem to get any better. What can I do?"

Let me allow Jesus to answer that for you. In the above story Jesus said, *"One thing is needful."* If you are willing to submit to what Jesus said—your life can be radically changed!

The Good Part

In Luke 10:42 Jesus said that Mary had *"chosen"* the one thing that was necessary to be an overcomer in life. Remember the word *chosen* means *choosing one out of many*. The one thing that Mary had chosen kept her from being worried and troubled in her mind. She must have continually chosen this one thing since the word means choosing one out of many. In other words, she had many things that came along in her life that could have worried her, made her feel uptight, hurt her feelings, discouraged her or caused her to be depressed. She could have allowed these things to put pressure on her until she was stressed out and felt like she was all tied up in knots. But each time a difficulty, crisis or problem arose in her life, she chose to dwell on the Word of God instead of the dilemma. That kept Mary walking in *peace* right in the midst of every storm, *victory* right in the midst of apparent defeat, and *joy* right in the midst of depressing times.

Jesus pointed out that because she made this choice every time, then that *"good part"* would not be taken away from her. And that is what Jesus was trying to get across to Martha.

Friend, it is *good* to have joy all the time. It is *good* to abide in peace no matter what is happening in your life. It is *good* to be strong and stable emotionally, regardless of what people do or don't do. It is *good* to have an optimistic outlook on life. It is *good* to approach every situation in life with a winner's attitude. And it is *good* to be and remain positive in spite of all the negatives that life will throw your way. But most of all, it is *good* to be hooked up with God and His Word—THAT IS YOUR LIFELINE!

When you choose that GOOD PART, then God's life will not be taken away from you! His life will lift you up above all the muck and mire of your life and cause you to soar with the eagles.

When we choose to do what Mary did, we too can live the good life! Glory Be To God!

CHAPTER

Times of Trouble

Now let's look at another example in the Bible that will help us to live free from stress and worry.

Turn to 1st Samuel, Chapter Thirty. Verse 1 tells us that David and his men had gone to the city of Ziklag. This was during the time period when Saul had been constantly pursuing David, trying to kill him. So David and his men (600 in number) had fled to the country of the Philistines. There, in the city of Gath, David found great favor with King Achish. King Achish gave David and his men the city of

Ziklag to live in and to possess. David lived there in the land of the Philistines for sixteen months.

We pick up the story here in 1st Samuel 30:1-4. David was returning to his home in Ziklag after being on a long trip. While he was away on the trip the Amalekites had invaded the city, burned it down and taken the women and children as captives. David's two wives were included in the capture. So when David and his men entered the city and found everything burned to the ground and all their wives, sons and daughters missing, it was not a happy time. Look at verse 4.

> **Then David and the people that were with him lifted up their voice and wept, until they had no more power to weep.**

Now think about their situation for a moment. They had just returned to their hometown only to find that their houses had been destroyed, their wives and children had been kidnapped and all their belongings had been stolen. I don't know about you but—

I would have cried too!

Listen, it is not wrong, or a sin, to cry. Remember, Jesus cried when Lazarus died (see John 11:35). There are times in our lives when this type of emotion is okay. But we must not remain there. That will only make matters worse. When things look dark and grim, it is time to bring in the light of God's Word to brighten our paths!

Let's see what happened in David's story. Verse 4 tells us that he cried until there were no more tears left to shed. Then the first part of verse 6 says:

> **And David was greatly distressed; for the people spoke of stoning him, because the soul of all the people was grieved, every man for his sons and for his daughters.**

Wow, I thought David's situation was already as bad as it gets. He had already lost his wives, home and belongings, but now all of his loyal men were bitter and enraged at him and were talking about stoning him to death! No wonder David was greatly distressed.

Have you ever been there? Or maybe you are there right now. It is a place where you feel all hell has broken loose. You feel like everything is caving in

around you. You feel like there is no way out of your mess. You feel distraught, discouraged and hopeless. You feel like life is not worth living anymore. You just want to give up and quit.

Listen friend, if that is where you are right now, or a place that you find yourself in frequently—God will not leave you nor forsake you. He has a way of escape for you! If you will look to Him He will lift you up. But you need to do just what David did.

David found himself in the worst situation that he could have ever imagined. There appeared to be no light at the end of the tunnel. It seemed that he was taking his last breath or hanging on by the final thread, so to speak. Literally everything seemed to be turning against David. BUT...

> *...but David encouraged himself*
> *in the Lord his God.*

What does it mean at the end of verse 6 when it says he *"encouraged himself in the Lord his God?"* Strong's Concordance gives the following definition for the word *encouraged*: *"to strengthen; to make strong; to restore to strength."* So, David *strengthened* himself in the Lord, he *restored his strength* and *made himself strong again* in the Lord his God.

<u>How Did He Do It?</u>

Many of the psalms that David wrote were written in the midst of troubling times. Let's take a look at some of them. As we read portions of them I believe that we will be able to see just how David became strong in the Lord even when everything around him was dictating failure, a time to worry, an occasion to be discouraged and plenty of reasons to quit.

Listen, if David could encourage himself in the Lord, then we can too! Why?—because God is no respecter of persons. What He's done for one He'll do for all.

So, let's see what David did. In Psalm 27:1 & 5, he said:

> **The Lord is my light and my salvation; whom shall I fear? The Lord is the strength of my life; of whom shall I be afraid? ⁵For in the time of trouble he shall hide me in his pavilion: in the secret of his tabernacle shall he hide me; he shall set me up upon a rock.**

For David to mention the *time of trouble* and not being *afraid*, shows us that he must have been facing some fearful and troubling times in his life. But he said that the Lord was his strength and hiding place; therefore he had no reason to be afraid or troubled.

Then in Psalm 28:7 he said:

> **The LORD is my strength and my shield; my heart trusted in him, and I am helped: therefore my heart greatly rejoices; and with my song will I praise him.**

Notice, David said in the above verses his strength came from the Lord. So he started speaking them out of his mouth and reminding himself of this truth. By getting his thoughts back on the Lord instead of his problems, he began drawing strength from God.

Another passage of scripture where David did this is Psalm 103:1-5.

> **Bless the LORD, O my soul: and all that is within me, bless his holy name. [2]Bless the LORD, O my soul, and forget not all his benefits: [3]Who forgives all your iniquities; who heals all your diseases; [4]Who redeems your life from destruction; who crowns you with loving-kindness and tender mercies; [5]Who satisfies your mouth**

**with good things; so that your youth is
renewed like the eagle's.**

He started out by talking to himself. That's right—he
talked to himself! He began telling his soul and
emotions something that would change the way he
was feeling. Obviously he must not have felt like
blessing the Lord, or he wouldn't have had to tell
himself to do it. And he even had to tell himself twice
to do it (see verses 1 and 2).

David reminded himself not to forget God's benefits.
Evidently he knew what they were but had
temporarily allowed the problems of life to
overwhelm him. So, he began reminding his soul
about the benefits of walking with his God.

Here is my paraphrase of what David said, *"God
forgives me for all my mistakes, He heals all of my
diseases, He pays the ransom for my life keeping me from
the pit of destruction, He fills my life with His love and
mercy and continually blesses me with good things. Then
He uses all of these benefits to renew strength within me
so that I will be strong and soar just like an eagle."*

Why did David start talking so positively? Could it
have something to do with, *"death and life are in the
power of the tongue?"* (Psalm 18:21) I like how The

Good News Translation renders this verse, *"What you say can preserve life or destroy it."* David must have had some understanding about putting the Word in his heart so that he could draw it up into his mouth when he needed it. The Psalmist said, *"Your word have I hid in mine heart, that I might not sin against you."* (Psalm 119:11)

In David's seemingly impossible situation he began drawing life from his God. He put himself in remembrance of the things that he knew by speaking them out of his mouth. This act of faith caused God's Word to start transferring Divine strength and life into David's heart, mind and body. Worry was replaced with peace, discouragement was replaced with boldness, and the desire to quit was replaced with an overcoming spirit. With this renewed strength from the Lord he was then able to say, *"Weeping may endure for a night, but joy comes in the morning."* (Psalm 30:5)

Notice, in the above verse David said, *"…joy comes."* How did it come to him? It came when he stirred himself up to meditate upon and speak out God's Word. This reminds me of what Nehemiah said, *"The joy of the Lord is your strength."* (Nehemiah 8:10)

You see, as David began dwelling on and speaking

God's thoughts, the transfer of strength that came from the Lord was accompanied by joy. But this joy was not natural human joy. It was the joy of the Lord! No wonder David was able to be strong again; he actually started making an exchange with the Lord. He exchanged his weakness for God's strength, his distress for God's joy.

The prophet Isaiah had something to say about this that will further enlighten us as to what David was doing. It's found in Isaiah 40:31.

> **But they that wait upon the LORD shall renew their strength; they shall mount up with wings as eagles; they shall run, and not be weary; and they shall walk, and not faint.**

Notice it says those that *"wait"* on the Lord. This Hebrew word means *to bind together or be joined to*. It doesn't mean that we are supposed to just sit around *waiting* to see if God is going to show up and do something. No, it means that we *join ourselves to* Him or *bind together with* Him. It goes on to say that by doing so we *"renew"* our strength. The word *renew* means *to change, substitute, alter, or change for the better*. Another way to say it would be to *"exchange."*

In essence, this is saying that we can alter our strength, substitute our strength, exchange our strength or change it for the better. Where is this new strength coming from? From the one to whom we are joined! We exchange our lack of strength for the Lord's strength! We get to substitute God's strength for our weakness. Wow, I would call that a change for the better!

This enhances our understanding of what David was doing as he was speaking the promises of God right in the midst of the storms of life. He was drawing power out of the unseen realm right into his present circumstances and situations, giving him the strength that he needed to overcome them.

Listen—what good would it have done for David to continue throwing a pity party? He had lost his city, his home, his wives, his friends and even his faithful employees. If he had waited a day or two until he had some more tears to shed, and then entered right back into weeping and grieving, it would have only taken him from one grief to the next. But David encouraged himself in the Lord. This got his focus off of himself and onto the Lord. It got his attention off of the problem and onto THE ANSWER.

Once David had made an exchange with the Lord,

his whole demeanor changed. He was now ready to go after what had been stolen from him. Notice what he said in 1st Samuel 30:8.

> **And David enquired at the LORD, saying, Shall I pursue after this troop? Shall I overtake them? And he [The LORD] answered him, Pursue: for you shall surely overtake them, and without fail recover all.**

Now that is encouraging—having the LORD say something like that to you right in the midst of apparent defeat. *"Go after your enemy now. You will overpower them and recover everything that you have lost."*

Would that help you? It sure would me. But David would never have heard from the Lord, had he not been exercising his faith in the Lord.

We know that he exercised his faith because God included him in Hebrews, Chapter Eleven. That chapter has been referred to as the "Hall of Faith." It mentions many individuals that used their faith in God to overcome in life, such as Abel, Enoch, Noah, Abraham, Sarah, Isaac, Jacob, Joseph, Moses and others. Then in verses 32-34 God says:

And what shall I more say? for the time would fail me to tell of Gideon, and of Barak, and of Samson, and of Jephthah; of <u>David also</u>, and Samuel, and of the prophets: [33]<u>Who through faith</u> subdued kingdoms, wrought righteousness, obtained promises, stopped the mouths of lions, [34]Quenched the violence of fire, escaped the edge of the sword, <u>out of weakness were made strong</u>, waxed valiant in fight, turned to flight the armies of the aliens.

Through faith David won battles and conquered his enemies. He received what God had promised him and was made strong when he felt weak. All because he decided to trust God and focus his attention on God's promises rather than the crisis he was facing or the setbacks of his life. By encouraging himself in the Lord he was able to renew his strength and be strong in the Lord. This positioned him to hear from heaven as to what he should do. And then when God told him to go defeat the enemy, he obeyed without hesitation. He knew that he wasn't going in his might or his power but God's. So, David went and recovered everything that had been stolen from him. Now look at 1st Samuel 30:18-19.

> **And David recovered all that the Amalekites had carried away: and David rescued his two wives. [19]And there was nothing lacking to them, neither small nor great, neither sons nor daughters, neither spoil, nor any thing that they had taken to them: David recovered all.**

And not only did David recover all that had been stolen, he even took all the flocks and herds of the enemy for himself—it was his reward for having faith in God (see Hebrews 11:6).

David received blessings because He obeyed and served the Lord his God. The promises of God came upon David because he refused to stay depressed, down or worried. David did not deny the problems of life, but faced them with the Lord's strength—and changed them! As he joined himself to the Lord, the battles became the Lord's battles, not his.

And listen, friend, when God is on your side and fighting for you—YOU WIN!

CHAPTER

Let the Lord Fight for You

As you learn to join yourself to the Lord in times of trouble, you will be able to hear God say the same thing He said to King Jehoshaphat. Look at what God said to him in 2nd Chronicles 20:15 & 17.

> **Thus says the LORD unto you, Be not afraid nor dismayed by reason of this great multitude; for the battle is not yours, but God's.**

> **¹⁷You shall not need to fight in this battle: set yourselves, stand still, and see the salvation of the LORD with you.**

Allow me to expound for just a moment about this statement that God made to Jehoshaphat. It goes right along with what we are studying.

By reading verses 1 – 13 of this chapter we can see that Jehoshaphat found himself in a crisis. The enemy was coming with a great multitude to destroy him. His situation looked bleak. It looked like there was no way out, and then verse 3 says that fear came. That means he was dealing with troubling thoughts and worry. But Jehoshaphat did exactly what we are supposed to do when we find ourselves worried or afraid. The end of verse 3 says that he *"set himself to seek the Lord."*

Then he stood up and began speaking things out concerning the Lord his God, and reminding God of His promises (verses 6-11). Then in verse 12 we see him stating the facts. He must have known that faith in his God could change those facts. In essence, he said in verse 12, *"Lord, we are not big enough nor are we smart enough in our own strength and in our own wisdom to overcome this situation that we are facing, so we get our eyes off of ourselves and look to you."*

Do you know what he was doing? He was doing exactly what we were talking about earlier in this book when we looked at 1st Peter 5:6-7. He was humbling himself by casting the worry and care of the apparent crisis upon the Lord, so that God could lift him up to victory! His faith then caused God to speak through the Prophet Jahaziel. God told Jehoshaphat that because he was focusing his attention upon Him and not the problem, He would fight Jehoshaphat's battles for him.

What if Jehoshaphat had continued to worry about the situation? Would he have been delivered from it? No. And this is where too many Christians are. They know what God has said about their troubles, but they don't humble themselves by getting their eyes off of themselves.

What if Jehoshaphat had started saying things like, "**I** can't handle this pressure. This is more than **I** can bear. What am **I** going to do? **I** just can't see any way out of this. No one else knows what **I'm** going through. Why is this happening to **me**? What have **I** done to deserve this? Why **me** God? **I** can't go on living like this!

I purposely made the word "I" and the word "me" bolder so that we can see where **OUR** problem is. Can you see how we enter into pride when things like that are spoken out of our mouths? It is definitely being self-centered. We must get our eyes off of ourselves—our inabilities, our weaknesses, our fears, our frustrations, our past failures, our lack and anything else that talks about me-me-me or I-I-I. The more we talk about ourselves the more limited we become. But when we talk about God—we take off all the limits!

Jehoshaphat began to magnify God when it looked like his whole life was going under. We have to do the same thing if we want to stay free from worry, stress, depression, discouragement, hurt feelings and strife. We MUST magnify God.

What does it mean to magnify God? Let me illustrate. If you take a magnifying glass and hold it above the words printed in your Bible, what does it do to the words? Someone may say, "It makes them bigger." But in actuality it does not make the words bigger at all; it just makes them APPEAR bigger in your eyes.

That is what we do when we magnify God. He is not changing or getting any bigger, but when we magnify Him our perception of Him changes. The more we magnify Him, the bigger He appears and the smaller our problems appear. And when we magnify God more than the problem, God is able to lift us up above our enemies.

That is what David did when he was right in the midst of his troubles. Look at what he said in the Psalms.

> **O magnify the LORD with me, and let us exalt his name together.** Psalm 34:3

> **I will praise the name of God with a song, and will magnify him with thanksgiving.** Psalm 69:30

Notice he magnified God by talking about Him rather than the problem. He praised, sang and gave thanks to God, which kept his eyes off of his problems as well as off of himself. Thus he kept himself clothed in humility instead of pride, which allowed God to lift him up out of his messes.

That is exactly what happened with Jehoshaphat. After Jehoshaphat and the people got their eyes on the Lord, and God had told them that He would fight their battles for them, Jehoshaphat made these statements: *"Have faith in the Lord your God and you will be able to stand strong. Have faith in His Prophets and you will have success."* Then Jehoshaphat chose people to sing praises to the Lord. Why did he do that? Because that kept their eyes off of their problems (and off of themselves) and kept them looking to God. They were magnifying God. Notice what happened in 2nd Chronicles 20:21-22.

> **And when he had consulted with the people, he appointed singers unto the LORD, and that should praise the beauty of holiness, as they went out before the army, and to say, Praise the LORD; for his mercy endures for ever. 22And when they began to sing and to praise, the LORD set ambushments against the children of Ammon, Moab, and mount Seir, which were come against Judah; and they were smitten.**

Listen, had they leaned to their own understanding they might have said, "This is crazy! How in the world is praising God going to change my situation? I'm about to be killed! I'm going under! If this faith business really worked then I wouldn't even be in this mess!"

It is quite possible that these kinds of thoughts were going through their minds. And had they spoken those things out, they surely would have been defeated. But when they began to sing and praise the Lord, God moved on their behalf. They had put themselves in a position where they placed their confidence in God, rather than focusing on their dilemma. They had joined themselves to God and His strength, rather than staying aligned with their problems.

What to Do In Your Midnight Hour

Look at Acts, Chapter Sixteen. The Apostle Paul had a vision one night. In the vision, a man appeared to him asking him to come to Macedonia. So Paul, along with his traveling companion Silas, headed to Macedonia. They ended up in the city of Philippi. There they cast an evil spirit out of a woman. The woman was a fortune-teller who made a lot of money for her masters. But when the spirit was cast out of her she could not tell fortunes any more. This upset her masters greatly because their profitable business scheme was now over. So they seized Paul and Silas, brought them to the city rulers and Roman officials and accused them of breaking Roman law. The authorities then commanded Paul and Silas to be whipped and cast into prison. After they had been severely beaten they were thrown into the inner dungeon of the prison and had their feet chained between large, heavy wooden blocks.

Now put yourself in their place for just a moment. You're in much pain from the beatings. You are exhausted physically and mentally. Everything around you points to the conclusion that *there is no way out of this mess!* What kind of thoughts would be going through your mind?

Paul and Silas were just as human as we are. Silas could have turned to Paul and said, "Paul, I thought you had a vision from God. Yeah, right—more like too much pizza before you went to bed. We are really helping the Christians here in Macedonia aren't we Paul? Ha! Look at us! Locked up, beaten up and I'm fed up! We've been serving God with our whole hearts and this is our reward? Where is God when we need him?"

Have you ever heard statements similar to those? Someone may say, "Yeah, Brother Larry, I've heard some of those things come out of my mouth!"

It is likely that we have all had our occasions of saying things that would be comparable—but we must not remain there. We must begin to magnify God. That is, we must begin to talk about Him and what He has to say, and quit talking about our problems and what they are trying to dictate to us.

Paul and Silas had plenty of cause to worry, get upset or be depressed. After all, what was going to happen to them next? Would they ever see their friends or family again? What would everyone think about them if they got out of prison—ex-cons! What would tomorrow hold? Would they die here in this prison? Would they be jerked out soon and stoned to death? Were they doomed to live the next 20-30 years as prisoners in this rat-infested dungeon? They could have worried about all these things and many more.

Let's see what Paul and Silas did when they faced what may have been the darkest hour of their lives.

Look at Acts 16:25-26.

> **And at midnight Paul and Silas prayed, and sang praises unto God: and the prisoners heard them. [26]And suddenly there was a great earthquake, so that the foundations of the prison were shaken: and immediately all the doors were opened, and every one's bands were loosed.**

What does this say they did? Does it say they cried and sang the blues? No, it says they prayed and sang praises. And as a result of their communication with God, He caused the very foundation of the prison to shake with such force that every door flew open and every prisoner's chains fell off of them.

What caused their situation to turn around? Was it positive thinking? How about meditation? NO! It was what they started speaking out of their mouths that caused their crisis to be turned into a victory. What did they start saying? Well, it says that they prayed and sang praises. That means they started talking to God and singing to Him. They probably started saying something like:

Father God, we thank you that your Word is true. You said that you would never leave us nor forsake us, so we thank you that you are right here with us. Lord, because you are our light and our salvation, then how could we be afraid of anyone? You are the strength of our lives; whom should we fear? Lord God, you are on our side, we will not fear what man can do to us. You are our Deliverer, our Helper, our Strengthener, our Comforter, our Healer, our Wisdom, our Peace and our Joy! We look to you and rejoice that we are counted worthy to suffer for your name's sake. We glory in tribulations that the power of God might be revealed in us. Who or what can separate us from your love, God? Nothing and no one can. Not tribulation, nor distress, nor persecution, nor famine, nor nakedness, nor peril nor sword. No! In all these things we are more than conquerors because of your love for us. Lord, your grace is sufficient to overcome every situation. Therefore we choose to be happy when we face weaknesses, insults, hard times, sufferings and all kinds of trouble for Christ. For when we are weak in our own human strength, then you enable, empower and divinely charge us with your strength. So Lord, we believe and say that we are strong in you and the power of your might! And we can do all things because of Christ's strength that abides in us! Hallelujah! Praise the Lord! Glory be to God! Thank you Jesus! Lord, you are good and your mercy endures forever!

Probably at this point their prayer turned into praise and worship. They found themselves singing to the Lord instead of crying and complaining about their predicament. They were magnifying God, not their problems. This showed God humility on their part, and enabled Him to exalt them—up above and out of their crisis.

I am reminded of something that the Apostle Paul said to the Corinthian church in 2nd Corinthians 4:8.

"We are troubled on every side but not distressed."

I read this passage from the New Living Translation and really liked it. Notice how it translates verses 8-9.

> **We are pressed on every side by troubles, but we are not crushed and broken. We are perplexed, but we don't give up and quit. ⁹We are hunted down, but God never abandons us. We get knocked down, but we get up again and keep going.**

I like that! We are not crushed or broken. We don't give up and quit. God never abandons us, and even when something happens in life that knocks us down, we get up again and keep going—not in our own strength, but in the strength of the Lord!

If we will make a decision to persevere and not give up when facing difficult times, but keep our eyes on the Lord and act upon His Word, then we will come out victorious every time!

You, my friend, can do the same thing that these men of God did. No matter what it is that you are facing, you can overcome it. You have the Greater One on the inside of you, so look to Him. Magnify Him and His Word. Praise Him, worship Him and give Him thanks for giving you the victory no matter what it looks like. Cast your frustrations, anger, hurts, cares, worries and concerns upon the Lord—He cares for you!

CHAPTER

The Alternative to Worry

We have already found out that God does not want us to worry. He wants us to cast our cares, concerns and worries upon Him. Obviously then, He must want us to live a carefree, stress-free and worry-free life.

Now just think about it for a moment... if you didn't have any worries, any concerns, or any cares to burden you or pull you down, what would life be like? Someone may say, "I would have peace of mind," or "my life would be peaceful."

That is exactly right! You would be at peace—with yourself, your spouse, your kids, your family, your friends, your coworkers, your in-laws and out-laws. In fact, you would be at peace with the whole world! But how do we get there? How do we turn our thoughts of something bad might happen, to something good is going to happen? WE MUST CHANGE THE WAY WE THINK!

"Oh Brother Larry, don't start on that positive thinking stuff." Don't worry, ☺ I won't. But I will show you what God has to say about our thoughts. Let's start in Romans 8:5-6.

> **For they that are after the flesh do mind the things of the flesh; but they that are after the Spirit the things of the Spirit. ⁶For to be carnally minded is death; but to be spiritually minded is life and peace.**

Notice, when we are carnally minded we don't walk in peace. A carnally minded person is one who is ruled by their senses and by human nature. Did you know that it is human nature to worry? Sure it is! Worrying about all the natural things is what we saw Martha doing when we looked at what Jesus said to her in Luke 10:38-42. However, this 6th verse in

Romans tells us that we can be spiritually minded, and by being so we will experience God's life and peace.

Look at how The Good News Translation renders these verses:

> **Those who live as their human nature tells them to, have their minds controlled by what human nature wants. Those who live as the Spirit tells them to, have their minds controlled by what the Spirit wants. ⁶To be controlled by human nature results in death; to be controlled by the Spirit results in life and peace.**

Notice, to be controlled by the Spirit means that we are living by what the Spirit tells us to do. Well, the Spirit always tells us to do things in line with the Word of God. So, when the Word of God controls our thoughts and actions, then we will live life to the fullest and be ruled by peace—not by worry, fear or all the other negative emotions that our flesh dictates.

The word *emotion* comes from a French word which means *to stir up,* and it comes from a Latin word which means *to remove or displace.* Now remember, emotions are not bad—Jesus showed emotions while He was on the earth and God has emotions too. In fact, God has given us HIS emotions. If you think about the fruits of joy and peace, they are in essence emotions. And when we *stir up* peace and joy, it *removes or displaces* us from the place of worry or discouragement. When we do so, we will live as the Spirit tells us to, and have our minds controlled by what the Spirit wants. Therefore our emotions will be positive and good.

But what about when we allow worry, strife, stress, etc. to *stir us up*—what does that do to us? It *removes or displaces* us from the place of peace and joy and the place where God can lift us up out of the problems of life.

Let me ask you a question. Do you have peace? Someone might say, "Oh, no way, I am an emotional wreck!"

But wait! Are you born again? Are you a child of God? Have you accepted Jesus Christ as your personal Lord and Savior? If so, then I have great news for you—you have God's peace living on the inside of you!

Look at Galatians 5:22-23.

> The fruit of the Spirit is love, joy, peace, longsuffering, gentleness, goodness, faith, 23Meekness, temperance: against such there is no law.

In this verse, Paul writes to the Church and tells us that there is fruit that we receive when we are born again and the Holy Spirit begins dwelling on the inside of us. Notice that peace and joy are listed in the top three! Peace and joy abide in us as Christians. Look at Romans 14:17.

> For the kingdom of God is not meat and drink; but righteousness, and peace, and joy in the Holy Ghost.

Did you see what this says? The Kingdom of God is righteousness, peace and joy in the Holy Ghost. And according to Luke 17:20-21 the Kingdom of God is on the inside of us!

> The kingdom of God comes not with observation: 21Neither shall they say, Lo here! or, lo there! for, behold, the kingdom of God is within you.

Glory to God! The Kingdom of God (righteousness, peace and joy in the Holy Ghost) is on the inside of me! Righteousness is dwelling in me! Peace is dwelling in me! Joy is dwelling in me!

So, anything that comes along in life that would make me feel unrighteous could not be truth, because God has already said that His righteousness is on the inside of me. Therefore, I am righteous regardless of how I feel.

Likewise, if I am facing some problem or situation with someone like a spouse or friend, and something is said or done that tries to rob me of my peace or take away my joy, then my responsibility is to be spiritually minded and allow truth to reign. If I let what others say and do control my emotions, regardless of their intentions, then I am allowing myself to be carnally minded. But if I choose to exercise my righteousness, peace and joy when unkind things are said or done, then I will operate in the peace of God and allow His life to dominate my emotions.

Here is something that EVERY child of God must learn if they want to be spiritually minded: *What people say or do does not determine whether I walk in peace and joy.* I am the only one who can choose how I am going to feel.

When something unkind is said or done to me, no one else chooses my thoughts. I alone choose my thoughts. And the thoughts I choose have a profound effect on my emotions. If I choose to dwell on thoughts of righteousness, peace and joy, then life and peace will dominate my feelings. But if I choose to worry or get frustrated or angry, then my feelings will be dominated by death and darkness.

Blame Shifting

"But Brother Larry, he hurt my feelings," or "she made me feel bad," or "they treated me like dirt," or "he embarrassed me," or "she didn't give me the time of day," or "they act like they don't like me," or "he doesn't ever listen to me," or "she always talks down to me," or "they don't treat me with any respect," or "he always makes me feel like I'm so stupid," or "she acts like I don't even exist." I could go on and on, but I think that these statements are a good sampling of the things that individuals think and say that cause them to fret, worry, get depressed, get upset or get angry with others.

Notice that all these statements are putting the blame for how I feel onto someone else. It is what they said or did, or what they didn't say or didn't do that caused me to be mad, depressed, worried, hurt, etc. But the truth is, they didn't *make me* feel this way. My feelings are totally controlled by my thoughts, regardless of the actions of others.

Remember in Luke 10:38-42 how Martha tried to blame Mary for her problems? Jesus let Martha know that Mary wasn't her problem. Jesus told her that her many worries were based on the fact that she was allowing herself to dwell on the wrong things.

We must quit blaming others and hold ourselves responsible for our feelings. I am the only one who can determine how I am going to feel. It doesn't matter what is said to me or what is done to me. Those things are not what determine my emotional state or the status of my feelings.

So the question becomes, how do I keep the feelings of rejection, worry, strife, etc. from overwhelming me, when I know what somebody did to me or said about me was wrong? How do I get to the place where I can control my emotions and keep them in line with righteousness, peace and joy? In other words, how do I become spiritually minded so that God's life and peace are dominating my emotions during those difficult times?

I believe that if you will go back and reread the previous chapters, you will find sufficient teaching that will answer these questions. But let's take a moment to review the things that will keep us operating in peace and joy.

1. As Peter said, humble yourself by casting your cares upon the Lord.
2. Like Mary did, choose to continually hear and act upon what God has said.
3. Like David did, encourage yourself in the Lord.
4. As Isaiah said, join yourself to the Lord and exchange your weakness for God's strength.
5. Like Jehoshaphat did, seek the Lord and let Him fight your battles for you.
6. As Psalms says, give thanks to the Lord and magnify Him instead of your problems.
7. Like Paul & Silas did, pray and sing praises when things are not going well.
8. Finally, become spiritually minded and allow righteousness, peace and joy to fill your cup to overflowing.

Doing the above things will cause us to be total overcomers in the realm of our emotions.

CHAPTER

God's Ways of Doing Things

Jesus had some additional things to say about overcoming the problems that are trying to defeat us. Let's take a look at some of them, beginning with Matthew 6:33.

> **Seek ye first the kingdom of God, and his righteousness; and all these things shall be added unto you.**

The "things" that Jesus is referring to in this verse are

monetary things. In the previous verses He mentions food and clothing, so we know He is talking about natural things. And we know that those natural things cost money. *Money problems have caused massive amounts of worry, strife, stress, etc. in people's lives.* Therefore, it would behoove us to take a closer look at this passage of Scripture.

It tells us to *seek first the Kingdom of God*. What is the Kingdom of God? Righteousness, peace and joy in the Holy Ghost! Where is the Kingdom of God? It is inside you! So, God tells us to seek righteousness, peace and joy that are already on the inside of us.

Let's dig into this verse a little bit. First of all, the word *kingdom* is the Greek word **basileia**. Vine's Expository Dictionary says, *"the term signifies the entire sphere of God's rule and action in relation to the world."* Strong's Concordance points out that it is *"not to be confused with an actual kingdom but rather the right or authority to rule over a kingdom."*

Jesus is pointing out that we are not to seek an actual kingdom. Instead, we are to seek our right and authority to rule the way that God rules and to act the way that God acts in our relations with people. Simply put, we are to seek God's ways of doing things here on the earth.

The verse goes on to say that we are also to seek *"his righteousness."* The word *righteousness* is the Greek word **dikaiosune**. Vine's says it *"is the character or quality of being right or just."* Vine's also points out *"it was formerly spelled 'rightwiseness', which clearly expresses the meaning."* That is very interesting, isn't it? Rightwiseness. That must mean that we are to be wise and do right.

Strong's Concordance gives the following definitions of the word righteousness: *"integrity, virtue, purity of life, rightness, correctness of thinking, feeling and acting."*

So what is God saying when He tells us to seek His righteousness? In essence He is saying, *"Seek my character and live by it. Make sure that your thoughts, feelings and actions are guided by integrity and goodness, and that you live a pure and right life."*

Now let's paraphrase the whole verse using what we have learned so far:

Make sure that you seek God. He has given you the authority to rule in this world with righteousness, peace and joy. And you are to do it just like Him, allowing integrity and goodness to define your character, and thereby living a life that is pure and honorable in front of all. If you do this, all the natural things that money can buy will be given to you.

Now here is the exciting part! God said that we are to "*seek*" to live this way. "Seek to live what way, Brother Larry?" Seek to reign in life just like God does! Seek to live in righteousness, peace and joy! Seek to live above our problems and not beneath them. Seek to live as the head and not the tail, to go over and not go under, to live as overcomers, more than conquerors, and victorious children of the most-high God!

In addition, Jesus told us in Luke 10:19 that He has given us authority to trample down every devil and demon that may attack us, and to exercise our authority over ALL the power of our enemies. Now let me ask you some questions. Is depression an enemy? Is worry an enemy? Is stress an enemy? How about low self-esteem, is it an enemy? Is fear an enemy? Are frustration, strife and uncontrolled anger enemies? What about offenses, do they treat us as a friend or foe? Listen, all of these things are meant to steal, kill and destroy, which lets us know that they are not our allies but our enemies.

If we put the verse here in Luke together with what Jesus said in Matthew 6:33, we can see clearly that we have authority and dominion to rule over all the power of the enemy. That means we have dominion over depression, fear, worry, strife, frustration, anger, discouragement, etc. We can rule over everything that wants to control our emotions. But I want you to notice, in Matthew 6:33, Jesus told us to seek to live this way. Strong's points out that to *seek* means: "*to seek [in order to find out] by thinking, meditating, reasoning, to enquire into.*"

This brings us right back to the thought realm! If we are going to seek righteousness, peace, joy and God's ways of doing things here on the earth, then we are going to have to *think* about them, *meditate* on them, and *enquire into* them. Jesus said that this type of seeking would even affect our financial affairs. That being the case, then if we seek after worry (that is we think about, meditate on, reason with and enquire into the cares of life) then our finances will be affected in the negative. In other words, things will be taken away from us! Whoa—we had better wake up to the devil's devices so he doesn't get an advantage over us (see 2nd Corinthians 2:11).

Let me reiterate what God said about seeking Him and His ways of doing things on the earth. He wants us to *seek, in order to find out, by thinking, meditating, reasoning and enquiring into* His thoughts and ways. Well, Jesus said in Matthew 7:7 that if we seek, we *"shall find!"* However, we must seek by doing it the way He has told us to do it. Seeking involves the mind and the will of man.

Let me give you an example. Let's say that your spouse does something or says something that is very offensive or hurtful to you. You now have to make a choice. You can let your flesh (your human nature) react to what just happened, which means your words and actions will correspond with being carnally minded. Or, you can let your heart (which contains God's nature) react to what just happened, which means your words and actions will correspond with being spiritually minded.

In other words, you can choose not to be offended or get mad. You can choose to believe the best in that person, and you can choose to stay in peace and let joy dominate your emotions. Remember, NO ONE CAN MAKE YOU HAVE NEGATIVE EMOTIONS. Your emotions are controlled 100% by what you are thinking about and meditating upon. And those thoughts are your choice—and yours alone.

Listen, we can actually get to the place in our walk with God that we can live a worry-free, stress-free, offense-free, depression-free and fear-free life. But we must seek! We must align our thoughts and our meditations with God's thoughts. Then our ways will line up with His.

"But Brother Larry, didn't the Prophet Isaiah say that God's thoughts and ways are much higher than man's thoughts and ways?" Yes he did. However, that passage of Scripture (Isaiah 55:8-13) also tells us that His Word contains His thoughts and ways, and that they can become ours. It tells us that when we think about God's Word and plant it in our hearts, it will act just like the rain or snow from heaven that waters the earth and brings forth a harvest. The seed of God's Word will bring forth a harvest of His thoughts and ways. In fact the 12th and 13th verses say that peace, joy and prosperity will be included in that harvest! Glory!

Now, let's go back to Matthew 6:33 concerning seeking God and His ways of doing things here on the earth. Reading the whole context of this passage (verses 19-34) really opened my eyes to some wonderful truths that pertain to our subject. God tells us in verses 19-24 to get our eyes, attention and focus off of money (that would include worrying about it). In verses 25-32 He tells us not to worry about all the things that life presents to us on a daily basis. In fact He gets pretty specific in verse 31 regarding what we tend to say when we are worried about things.

Therefore take no thought, saying, What shall we eat? or, What shall we drink? or, Wherewithal shall we be clothed?

In essence He says, don't say things like, "What are we going to do about this? What are we going to do about that? I don't know what we should do about..." Worry, worry and worry some more! He is saying, "Stop that worrying!"

Notice, He said don't *"take"* the thoughts. This is where many Christians get into trouble. We must realize that thoughts of doubt, depression, worry, discouragement, fear, frustration, stress, strife, etc. are going to come to all of us. But it is what we do with those thoughts that will determine our state of mind, our mental health or our emotional well-being.

So God says *"don't take"* those wrong thoughts. But how do you not take them? Look at the verse, He says, *"Take no thought saying..."* In other words, "Don't speak those thoughts out of your mouth." He is letting us know that thoughts are controlled by words.

> *It has been said that a thought left unspoken is a thought that dies unborn!*

But listen, it is not enough just to refrain from saying the negative thoughts. That is why God continues in verse 33 by telling us to seek Him and His ways. Remember, to seek deals with the thought realm. So if we are thinking about God's Word, we must take it one step further by speaking God's Word out of our mouths. That causes us to take God's thoughts and replace the negative ones.

We take thoughts by speaking them.

Someone may ask, "What does it mean to take a thought?" It means that we have allowed the thought to remain in our mind—to the point where it affects the way we act.

When we allow thoughts of anger, worry, etc. to remain in our mind, we end up taking those thoughts by speaking them. Then our words and actions become negative, pessimistic and even hurtful ones. Taking those kinds of thoughts will cause us to complain, find fault, accuse others, etc. But even worse than that, taking them will hinder God from being able to help us.

In other words, if we are thinking and speaking the wrong things then we are not in faith, we are not pleasing to God, and we are not in a position to receive any help from Him. That is the place where uncontrolled emotions run rampant. Stress, anger, depression, hurt feelings, hopelessness, seemingly unbearable pressure, and many other emotions begin taking their toll on our mental health. This results in other areas of our lives being affected as well. Left unchecked, these emotions and feelings can be detrimental to our physical well-being, harmful to our relationships with others, and very destructive to our finances.

However, just the opposite is also true! If we control our emotions by thinking God's thoughts and acting just like He does in all the various situations that we encounter in life, then righteousness, peace and joy will take over. Then our feelings and emotions will be beneficial to our health, enhance our relationships with others, and even improve our financial status.

No wonder God deals with worry and the thought realm in this passage of Scripture. It is vital to our lives! Again, verse 33 in essence says that we are to take God's thoughts and His ways and apply them to everyone with whom we have contact here on the earth.

Then in verse 34 God concludes this passage by saying:

Take therefore no thought for the morrow: for the morrow shall take thought for the things of itself. Sufficient unto the day is the evil thereof.

The Living Bible reads, *"So don't be anxious about tomorrow. God will take care of your tomorrow too. Live one day at a time."* The Good News Translation says it this way, *"So do not worry about tomorrow; it will have enough worries of its own. There is no need to add to the troubles each day brings."*

Let me reiterate something I said earlier in this book. *Worry does not empty tomorrow's problems; it just empties today's strength.*

Listen, if you start worrying about what is going to happen tomorrow (meaning tomorrow, next week, next month, etc.) then your heart becomes overcharged. That allows the thorns of all the cares to choke the Word out of you, and then you get pulled down into the muck and mire of life. This is what causes you to be ZAPPED of the strength that you need to face TODAY'S problems! Then one or more of the following symptoms will be evident in your life: You'll just want to sleep or lie around and do nothing, or you will have headaches or other bodily ailments, or you will be grumpy and hard to live with, or feel like you have no purpose in your life—the list goes on and on.

Listen, the fact that God uses all these verses to talk about our thoughts shows us that this is vitally important! We must think about and mediate upon God's thoughts and ways, and then begin speaking them out of our mouths so that we take hold of them. Don't take hurtful thoughts by speaking them, but do take God's thoughts by speaking them.

Allow me to share Matthew 6:33-34 from the Message Bible.

> **Steep your life in God-reality, God-initiative, God-provisions. Don't worry about missing out. You'll find all your everyday human concerns will be met. [34]Give your entire attention to what God is doing right now, and don't get worked up about what may or may not happen tomorrow. God will help you deal with whatever hard things come up when the time comes.**

In essence, this says to soak, immerse or saturate your life in God-reality (that's God's thoughts or truth), God-initiative (that's God's plans and His ways), and God-provision (that's looking to Him as your provider). Keep your thoughts and meditations on what God is doing now. Don't get worked up about what may or may not happen tomorrow. God will take care of that too!

Isn't that a good translation of this verse? I think so. Notice the part that says, *"Don't get worked up about what may or may not happen tomorrow."* This is where so many are defeated. They allow their imaginations to run wild! They imagine the worst, and yet God gave us our imaginations to imagine the best!

Let's talk about the word *imagination* for a moment. The Merriam-Webster's Online Dictionary defines it as follows:

1. The act or power of forming a mental image of something not present to the senses or never before wholly perceived in reality.
2. Creative ability; ability to confront and deal with a problem; the thinking or active mind.
3. A creation of the mind... fanciful or empty assumption.

So, imaginations are mental pictures formed by our thoughts and meditations. If our thoughts and meditations are focused on our Father God and His Word, then our God-formed imaginations will have the creative ability to confront, deal with, and overcome every problem that we face. Positive imaginations will cause us to speak and release the power of life, giving us an assurance that everything is going to be fine—even before our senses wholly perceive it in the physical realm.

However, when our thoughts and meditations are focused on our problems and what everybody else is thinking or doing, then our minds will create *fanciful and empty assumptions*. We will then say things that release the power of death. This opens the door for worry, stress or pressure that will hinder us from confronting and dealing with the problems. Those *false mental images* will keep us bound, even though most of them will never come into reality. They are *empty assumptions* that rob us of our peace and joy and keep us from acting in righteousness.

Worry is nothing more than perverted imagination

The devil does not want us to use our God-given imaginations for their intended purpose. Why? Because he knows that if we are imagining that everything God has said to us and about us is happening, then we will be talking and acting like it, and our faith will bring it into reality. So the devil wants to pervert our imaginations and try to get us to think about and meditate on the wrong things. He wants us to worry, get upset, and be depressed, etc. because that puts him in a position to steal, kill and destroy.

So we must control our thoughts. Let's shut the door on (carnally minded) thoughts that would upset, offend or hurt us, and take hold of (spiritually minded) thoughts that will bring us life and peace.

CHAPTER

Supernatural Peace of Mind

Let's look at some more Scriptures that will help us reach our goal of being spiritually minded. Look at Psalm 119:165.

> **Great peace have they which love your law** [the Word] **and nothing shall offend them.**

"Great peace" — would you like some of that? If so,

then you must love the Word. And according to Jesus in John 14:15, 21 & 23, if you love God's Word then you will *be a doer of it*. And in order to be a doer of it, you must *know it*. And if you want to know it, you must spend sufficient time *reading, thinking, meditating upon and speaking it*. Then when you know it, the Word will make you free! (See John 8:32.)

Listen, you won't walk in great peace just because you read through your Bible in one year! Now don't take me wrong, that is fine if you choose to do that. However, that will not be enough for you to be an overcomer in this life. Notice what God said in Deuteronomy 6:6-7.

> **And these words, which I command you this day, shall be in your heart: ⁷And you shall teach them diligently unto your children, and shall talk of them when you sit in your house, and when you walk by the way, and when you lie down, and when you rise up.**

Let me paraphrase that for you. *You must fill your heart with God's Word. Then give constant attention to telling your children what God says in His Word. Teach them what it says when you are sitting around in your home and also when you are out running errands. Make sure they hear the Word every night when they go to bed, and put it in their ears at the breakfast table every morning.*

Listen, if we are constantly speaking and teaching the Word to our children (morning, afternoon and night) then what do you suppose we are going to be thinking about? What do you think we are going to be meditating upon? And if we are constantly speaking them, what thoughts are we taking hold of? Obviously we would be studying, learning, thinking about, meditating upon, speaking and acting upon God's thoughts and ways. In other words, we would be seeking first the Kingdom of God and His righteousness! And that, my friend, will keep us operating in righteousness, peace and joy in the Holy Ghost!

Not only that, but our children will grow up being spiritually minded! They will have total control of their emotions. No more low self-esteem. No more depression. No more staying offended when offense comes. No more worries, cares, anxieties or stress.

When they learn to exercise their authority and dominion, they will be able to ward off pressure situations and remain in peace and keep their joy. Wow! What a way to be raised! Better yet—what a way to live!! Do you think it is possible? Absolutely! It's possible for us and our kids too!

So again, God said that we would have great peace if we would hear and do the Word. Then He said that nothing should offend us. In other words, when we love the Word we are enveloped or surrounded with great peace, and that peace wards off all offenses.

God's peace defends us against hurt feelings, protects us against unforgiveness, deflects wrong thoughts from us and holds off or keeps at bay all the things that would cause us to stumble and fall in our Christian walk.

Let's see what else God has to say about His peace. Look at Isaiah 26:3.

> **You** [God] **will keep him in perfect peace whose mind is stayed on you: because he trusts in you.**

Let's read this verse from the Amplified Bible. *"You* [Lord] *will guard him and keep him in perfect and constant peace whose mind [both its inclination and its character] is stayed on You, because he commits himself to You, leans on You, and hopes confidently in You."*

How would you like to have perfect and constant peace? God tells us how to get it right here in this verse. He says our minds have to be fixed, focused and remain on Him. Take a look at Young's Literal Translation. It says, *"An imagination supported Thou fortifiest peace—peace! For in Thee it is confident."* In other words, when our imaginations are supported by God's thoughts and ways, God reinforces His peace within us. Then our confidence in Him remains strong.

Now look at Philippians 4:6-8.

> **Be careful for nothing; but in every thing by prayer and supplication with thanksgiving let your requests be made known unto God. [7]And the peace of God, which passes all understanding, shall keep your hearts and minds through Christ Jesus. [8]Finally, brethren, whatsoever things are true, whatsoever things are honest, whatsoever things are just, whatsoever things are pure, whatsoever things are lovely, whatsoever things are of good report; if there be any virtue, and if there be any praise, think on these things.**

Earlier in this book we looked at verse 6 and found out that God said for us not to worry or be troubled with cares about anything. But He continues in this sixth verse by telling us to constantly talk to Him about all the things in life that we are going through (that's the prayer and supplication part).

That does not mean that we complain, whine or protest to God about being in the test or trial. Our prayers shouldn't include things like, "Why me, God?" or "God, my life was a whole lot easier before I started walking by faith," or "What have I done to deserve this?" or "God, where are you, I don't feel like you are with me," or "Oh God, I just don't think I can take this anymore." These things may indeed be how we are feeling, but expressing those things will not open the door for God to change our situations. Remember, speaking out those negative feelings will cause us to *take* thoughts that will be harmful to our lives.

Notice, the verse says that our prayers and supplications are to be made *"with thanksgiving."* This indicates that there is expectancy in our prayers. We are expecting God to hear and answer our prayers, so we give Him thanks. We are not giving Him thanks for the problem because this verse says, *"in everything"* not *"for everything."* This means that in every situation we are going through, we are to look to Him and give Him thanks for the answer.

In essence, this verse tells us that we are supposed to look to God to see what He has to say about our problem, believe what He has said and then repeat His words back to Him. After that, we give Him thanks for hearing and answering our prayers. That keeps us from getting worried, uptight or anxious about it.

Think about how wonderful this is—God tells us not to worry when we are facing troubling times, then gives us the words to speak about the difficulties, and finally tells us to give Him thanks for taking care of them. Now listen, that takes faith because we have to take *self* out of the equation. We can't worry. We can't think and speak our own thoughts and ways. And we can't complain and talk negatively. We must cast our cares upon Him. We must pray and speak His Word. And we must give Him thanks for taking care of everything for us. That's faith in action!

Actually, what we are doing is what we read previously in Isaiah 26:3—we are trusting Him right in the middle of the crisis and therefore keeping our minds fixed on Him. That brings His perfect peace into the difficult situations. Then His peace is able to surpass our natural thinking process and guard our hearts and minds against fear, worry, torment, etc., which is what Philippians 4:7 tells us. In fact, verse 7 tells us the result of being doers of verse six: *"and the peace of God, which passes all understanding, shall keep your hearts and minds through Christ Jesus."* In other words, God's peace transcends or goes way beyond our natural understanding. Then that peace guards our hearts and minds because we are in unity with Jesus and His anointing.

Now think about this for a moment. Since God said, *"Don't worry or have anxiety about anything"* then we can do it! It would be unfair and unjust of God to tell us to do something if we were not capable of doing it. Therefore, since God has commanded us to *not worry*, then we can choose to *not worry*!

Let's look again at John 14:27.

> **Peace I leave with you, my peace I give unto you: not as the world gives, give I unto you. Let not your heart be troubled, neither let it be afraid.**

Remember, when God said, *"let not your heart be troubled"* we saw that the word means *to cause one inward commotion, or take away his calmness of mind.* It also means *to stir up, render anxious or distressed*. And God says to *not let* our emotions be that way. He goes on to say, *"neither let it be afraid."* The word *afraid* means *cowardly, timid or fearful*.

We are not supposed to let things cause us inward commotion or take away our calmness of mind. We have to make a choice to *not let* things stir us up, render us anxious or cause us to be stressed out. And we must decide not to be cowardly (running from our problems), nervous or intimidated (because of who we are around) or fearful (of failure or rejection). God said, DON'T DO IT!

Now here is the exciting part. Before God told us in this verse to take total control of our emotions, He gave us some supernatural equipment. He said, I GIVE YOU MY PEACE AND I AM LEAVING IT WITH YOU. What did He give us and what did He leave with us? His peace! HIS PEACE—HIS PEACE—HIS PEACE! Not the world's peace but His and His alone! Hallelujah! God gave me His peace. He left it with me so that I would have the means to ward off all worry, hopelessness, strife, stress, depression, anger, hurt feelings, fear, etc.

In the context of this verse, God lets us know that because He has given us His peace, then we can have complete control over our mind and emotions. We can always keep our composure, be relaxed and stay calm. We can direct our minds to stay quiet and undisturbed. We can live in serenity and a state of tranquility.

"Oh, Brother Larry, I would love to live that way."

THEN YOU MUST BELIEVE WHAT GOD HAS SAID AND START ACTING LIKE IT IS TRUE, BECAUSE IT IS!

Let's go back to Philippians 4 and look at the eighth verse. We have already looked at verses 6 and 7 where God tells us how to get His peace to ascend above all our worries, anxieties and cares. (And once again, since He said to do it—then we can do it!) Then he tells us in verse 8 what our imaginations and thoughts ought to be based on.

> **Finally, brethren, whatsoever things are true, whatsoever things are honest, whatsoever things are just, whatsoever things are pure, whatsoever things are lovely, whatsoever things are of good report; if there be any virtue, and if there be any praise, think on these things.**

In essence God tells us what we must keep our minds fixed upon in order to have His perfect peace operative in our lives.

Let me give you my paraphrase of this verse. *Our thoughts should ALWAYS be thoughts of—whatever is truth, whatever is honorable, whatever is righteous, whatever is pure, whatever is pleasing, and thoughts that will promote positive and favorable speaking. Besides that, we should think on things of moral excellence and include thoughts of commendation, admiration and appreciation.*

God said, *"think on these things."* That means we can do it! We can—we can—we can! In fact, a few verses later (verse 13) He said we can! *"I can do all things through Christ because His strength is inside of me!"* Hallelujah! I can keep my mind on all those things. I can cast all my cares, worries and burdens upon Him. I can walk in supernatural peace everyday of my life regardless of what somebody says or does, and no matter what is going on around me.

Wow! This sounds like life is going to be a whole lot more fun and enjoyable! Yes—Yes—A thousand times yes! If God said it then WE CAN have it in our lives! Therefore, we must make the decision to be *doers* of God's Word. If we are just a *hearer* or even a *"tryer"* of God's Word, it won't work. But when we act upon His Word, then everything we do will be blessed! (See James 1:25.)

CHAPTER

Our Emotions—Redeemed!

This next Scripture will help you to see why it is possible for us to walk in God's divine peace.

Look at Isaiah 53:4-5.

> **Surely he [Jesus] has borne our griefs, and carried our sorrows: yet we did esteem him stricken, smitten of God, and afflicted. ⁵But he was wounded for our transgressions, he was bruised for our iniquities: the chastisement of**

our peace was upon him; and with his stripes we are healed.

The Hebrew word for *griefs* means *sickness,* referring specifically to *physical sickness.* The Hebrew word for *sorrows* means *pains and sorrows* and refers to both the *physical and emotional realm.* So what does it mean when it says that Jesus has borne our physical sicknesses and pains and also carried our emotional sorrows and pains? The Hebrew word used for *hath borne* means *to take away or carry off,* and the word used for *carried* means *to bear a load.* So this verse is telling us that Jesus became our substitute! He took and carried away all of our sicknesses, and already bore or endured the load of all our pains—both physical and emotional!

Now notice what was said in the 5th verse. *"...the chastisement of our peace was upon him."* What does that mean? The Amplified Bible says, *"...the chastisement [needful to obtain] peace and well-being for us was upon Him."*

In other words, Jesus took all of our pandemonium, upheaval, turmoil, chaos, uproar, confusion, madness, rage, fury, panic, fear, terror and every other type of mental disturbance. Simply stated, *He took all of our emotional disorders for us!* Now we can have emotional order. In other words, we can have our emotions controlled by peace and joy.

Let's take just a moment to discuss both the Greek and Hebrew definitions of this word *peace*. In Philippians 4:7 (where God tells us how to get His peace to ascend above all our worries) the Greek word used is *eirene*. Strong's Concordance says that it means: *"harmony, concord, security, safety, prosperity (because peace and harmony make and keep things safe and prosperous)."* W. E. Vine's Expository Dictionary says that this peace is the *"sense of rest and contentment."* Vine's also points out that the corresponding Hebrew word is *shalom*, *"which primarily signifies wholeness."*

The word *shalom* is used here in Isaiah 53:5 where it says, *"the chastisement of our peace was upon Him."* Strong's defines this word as: *"completeness (in number), safety, soundness (in body), welfare, health, prosperity, peace, quiet, tranquility and contentment."* In other words, it takes in the complete spectrum of man—spiritually, mentally, physically, financially and socially.

Just think—Jesus took our emotional disorders upon Himself so that we didn't have to, and then He gave us His peace or *His mental and emotional stability!* Glory to God! That means we can keep our emotions stable and we can remain in peace even in the most troubling of times.

I am reminded of some things that David said in the Psalms.

> **For in the time of trouble he shall hide me in his pavilion: in the secret of his tabernacle shall he hide me.**
> (Psalm 27:5)

> **You are my hiding place; you shall preserve me from trouble; you shall compass me about with songs of deliverance. Selah.** (Psalm 32:7)

It sounds to me like David had troubles just like we do! But notice what he did in those times of trouble. He began speaking things out about His God. He got his eyes off of his problems and onto his answer. He looked to God as a shelter and hiding place. And we are supposed to be doing the same thing!

Let me give you an illustration. If you were facing some horrendous situations, all hell had broken loose in your life, and you felt like everything that could go wrong was coming against you all at once—then suddenly God appeared (where you could see Him and touch Him) and said, "My child, hurry over here and hide behind me. I will take care of all of this for you." What would you do?

Well of course you would rush over and quickly get behind Him and hold on to Him. And just what do you think would begin to overwhelm your mind, thoughts and emotions? I suppose you would start thanking Him for His help. Your words would probably turn to praise and worship. Your thoughts would no longer be negative, nervous, worrisome, distraught, troubled or upset. You would more than likely find your mind and emotions in a state of tranquility, quiet and calm. In fact, you might even find yourself peeking around God and laughing at the problems you were facing, maybe saying things like, "You can't get to me now—Ha, Ha, Ha!" It would bring you complete peace—a peace that went way beyond your natural understanding.

Can you see what happens when your emotions are under control? Your emotional order (having your emotions under control) would cause your reactions to the problems to be very different. *You would find yourself operating in peace right in the middle of the storm, remaining stable when the outburst comes at you, and being at rest in every difficult situation.*

"Well Brother Larry, if God appeared to me like in your illustration, it would be easy to control my emotions."

Do you know what? If we make a statement like that then we are no better off than doubting Thomas. He said that unless he could use his physical senses to confirm the reality of Jesus, he would not believe. And when Jesus appeared to Thomas and the disciples He told Thomas that his words and actions had no faith involved in them and therefore would receive no blessings. You can read about it in John 20:24-29. And in the 29th verse Jesus tells us that the ones who are going to receive His blessings are those of us who believe without having to see: "...*blessed are they that have not seen, and yet have believed.*"

Now listen, if you want to walk in supernatural peace and have total control of your emotions, then you must believe (and act upon) all the Scriptures that we have looked at in this book. IT IS GOD'S WORD AND IT IS TRUTH! In fact, it is truer than your problems. Your problems are facts that can be changed. But God's Word is forever settled, it will never pass away and it is the truth that never changes!

When we put our trust in God and what He has said, then He becomes our shelter or hiding place just like

He did for David. In fact, wisdom tells us in Proverbs 1:33 that if we obey her (that means that we act like God's Word is true whether it looks like it or not) then she will cause us to be safe and secure and free from all fear. We are told in Proverbs 18:10 that the righteous are to use the name of the Lord. It becomes their strong tower and safe haven. David said almost the same thing in Psalm 61:3.

For thou hast been a shelter for me, and a strong tower from the enemy.

I don't know if you have your shoutin' clothes on or not. But if you don't, I suggest you put down this book and go change clothes. Go put your shoutin' clothes on, because what I'm getting ready to share is going to make you wanna' shout!

Proverbs 18:10 says the name of the Lord is a *"strong tower."* David said in Psalm 61:3 that the Lord was a *"strong tower"* from the enemy. As I studied the Hebrew word for *tower* I found these definitions among the list: *an elevated stage or a raised bed.*

Did you hear that? The Lord is a *raised bed* for us toward our enemies. A bed indicates a place where you lay down and rest. And the word *raised* indicates *up above* something. What is this saying? It is saying that when we trust God and act upon His Word He *lifts us up above our enemies* (problems, hurts, disappointments, frustrations, worries and cares) and *lays us on His bed of peace*. We can look down from that position of rest and do just like God does at his enemies—laugh, laugh and laugh some more (see Psalms 2:4, 37:12-13 & 59:8). Okay, you can shout now if you want to!

Notice that Proverbs 18:10 says, *"the name of the Lord is a strong tower; the righteous run into it and are safe."* The Hebrew word for *safe* means *to be too high for capture*. Oh—Glory! When God lifts me up, He lifts me up so high that my enemies can't capture me. He puts me out of their reach inside His strong tower and then I can remain in peace as I lay upon that raised bed. Maybe it really is true that we can *"float through life on flowery beds of ease!"*

Now don't think that I'm implying that you aren't going to face any problems in life. Haven't you noticed the many Scriptures we have examined? They ALL indicate that the reason God gave us His peace is because we are going to be confronted with many situations that could throw our emotions into disarray. However, if we face those situations armed with God's supernatural equipment, we can overcome them every time!

Look at what Jesus said in John 16:33.

> **These things I have spoken unto you, that in me you might have peace. In the world you shall have tribulation: but be of good cheer; I have overcome the world.**

He said that He has spoken (His Word) to us so that we can have His supernatural peace. Where and when did He say that we can have this peace? *"In the world..."* Did you hear that? We can have His peace right here on the earth even when we are facing tribulation.

The Greek word for *tribulation* means *pressure, oppression, affliction, distress, difficulties, troubles and problems.* Wow—I can activate supernatural peace (the same peace that Jesus had) right in the midst of all my difficult times.

That is why Jesus went on to say, *"be of good cheer."* The Greek says that we are to *be bold and courageous.* When does this verse indicate that we are to be bold, courageous and cheerful? While going through all the tests and trials of life! And what gives us the right to do that? Jesus tells us at the end of the verse: *"I have overcome the world."* That means that Jesus has defeated all our enemies, including those that come against our minds or emotions.

So, we can boldly declare that Jesus has already defeated our problems; therefore we are going to remain in peace. Praise the Lord! The chastisement of our peace was upon Him. Somebody ought to shout "Hallelujah!"

Now let's go back to John 14:27 for just a moment. Remember, Jesus said, "...*my peace I give to you, <u>not as the world gives</u>...*" What does He mean by that? Well, ask yourself the question, "How does the world give peace?" The answer is: When everything is peaceful, then we can have peace.

If there are terrorists at work, then people don't have peace. If snipers or serial killers are on the loose, then people lose their peace. If there is war, people are robbed of their peace. If there are catastrophes, then people can't find their peace. If the stock market crashes, people watch their peace vanish. If a spouse or friend mistreats them, then many people take offense and allow their peace to fly away like a bird.

In other words, *the world's peace is governed entirely by what is going on around us, whereas God's peace is governed entirely by what is going on inside us!*

The world's peace is governed by how *others choose to act*, but God's peace is governed by how *we choose to act*. The difference between the two is like night and day, or light and dark. That's because the world's system of peace is part of the kingdom of darkness, whereas God's system of peace is part of the kingdom of light.

Listen, those of us who are born again (those who have accepted Jesus Christ as their personal Lord and Savior) are called the children of light (Luke 16:8, Ephesians 5:8 & 1st Thessalonians. 5:5). So let's start acting like it! It is time for us to grow up and quit allowing ourselves to be bothered by what other people do.

I will reiterate something that I said earlier in this book—NO ONE CAN MAKE YOU MAD, MAKE YOU FEEL GUILTY, MAKE YOU FEEL DUMB, MAKE YOU FEEL INTIMIDATED OR MAKE YOU FEEL ANY OTHER WAY! We alone are the ones who choose how we are going to feel—period! It doesn't matter what other people say nor do, we still have to make a choice. Are we going to react according to our flesh or be Spirit-led? If we are full of God's Word we will be spiritually minded and respond accordingly.

When we are minding the things of God we will do the following: Humble ourselves and cast our cares upon the Lord; keep our thoughts on true, pure and lovely things; not allow ourselves to be overcharged; magnify God instead of the problems; encourage ourselves in the Lord; be bold about our peace of mind; let God be our strong tower and hiding place; believe that Jesus already took everything that could rob us of our peace; imagine only good things; love the Word more than the offenses; stop speaking (and thereby taking) negative thoughts when they come; seek to live in righteousness, peace and joy; join ourselves to the Lord (exchanging our strength for His); pray and sing praises to God (at all times); and finally, let the Lord fight our battles for us.

Wow! That is a mouthful. It is one long (very long) sentence! Now—STOP—and please take a moment to re-read the last two paragraphs, because they summarize the message of this book.

CHAPTER

Why Am I Acting Like This?

Up until this point, we have discussed the exercising of control over our feelings, when circumstances people, or the devil try to dictate how we are going to feel and act. In other words, we have discussed things that come from outside the body that try to influence our minds and emotions. But what about things that are happening *inside the body*—what effect can they have on our feelings, and can we exercise control over them?

Let's list some things that we might experience in our lives, concerning our physical bodies, which could influence the way we feel.

➤ Being in pain
➤ A woman's menstrual cycle
➤ Being on medication
➤ Not getting enough sleep
➤ Hormonal changes
➤ Being physically exhausted

All of these things can have enormous effects on the emotions of individuals. Obviously, some of them greater and some of them lesser; nonetheless, they will confront us (male or female) at some point in our lives. There is no denying that going through these challenges or experiencing these physical conditions can influence your emotions.

When someone is in pain, it is hard for them to think about others and not act in an unselfish way. Sometimes ladies experience major mood swings at certain points of their menstrual cycle, and find themselves speaking harsh words to particular people. While people are on medications, their bodies can be altered to the point where they don't think clearly, and then they end up saying or doing things in an unkind way. When the human body doesn't get enough sleep, it can be thrown into a tailspin, making it hard for the person to exercise joy. Hormonal changes taking place in the human body can affect the brain's normal thinking pattern, and then the individual has an inclination to let their peace fly away. And finally, physical exhaustion can make it difficult for one to be patient and/or gentle with people.

All of these things are real scenarios that we face as human beings. So the question becomes, can we still maintain control over our feelings when our bodies are undergoing these challenges?

I am reminded of a statement that's been attributed to a man of God by the name of Smith Wigglesworth. Someone had walked up to him and asked him how he felt. He quickly asserted, "I never ask Smith Wigglesworth how I feel, I tell him how I feel!"

Of course, Brother Wigglesworth would not have had to deal with the same physical problems that a woman would. However, I'm absolutely sure that since he was just as human as the rest of us, he did have to deal with some of the other issues we have discussed.

Is it possible that he knew something that we don't?

Could it be that we have more authority over our bodies than we actually realize? And if so, can we exercise authority and dominion over our bodies even when all of these things that we discussed are going on inside of them?

Further still, which one of these physical problems gives us the right to treat someone else in an ungodly way? Do we have a right to stir up strife and walk out of love due to one of these things? Proverbs 17:19 and 28:25 say the person that stirs up strife is full of pride and loves sin.

When a physical problem is going on in our bodies, do we have the right to put others down behind their back because of something they did? Are we EVER entitled to hate, hold onto unforgiveness, envy, be bitter toward or slander others? First Corinthians 3:3 tells us that this is being carnal. Second Corinthians 12:20-21 calls it sin. And Galatians 5:19-21 calls these actions works of the flesh, and categorizes them right along with adultery, witchcraft and even murder!

Do we have the right because of physical problems to throw pity parties or dive into discouragement or depression? Are we acting righteously when we wear our feelings on our shirt sleeves, or are we exempt from acting right because of these problems?

Now please don't get mad at me. I'm just asking these questions so that we can examine them in the light of God's Word, and not according to our natural human reasoning.

We have previously looked at numerous Scriptures where God revealed that He has already delivered us from all emotional disorder, and that He has given us His supernatural peace and joy. (Supernatural means that God uses His super to change our natural.)

So my question is, *can we or can we not use God's peace and joy when we are facing these physical challenges?*

Someone, male or female, may say, "Well, I just can't help it. I'm going through this stage of life or having this physical problem, and I just can't help the way I feel or act."

Alright, let's assume for just a moment that the above statement is true. If you and I cannot help the way we feel and act when facing certain physical problems, then we have to ask ourselves, "In which of life's situations will God's Word work for us, and in which ones will it not work? Which of these physical conditions rightfully empower us to be unkind, act selfishly, speak harshly, sow discord, walk out of love, disregard God's fruits of peace and joy, etc.?"

Do any of these conditions actually excuse us from acting upon God's Word? Ephesians 4:29 says, *"Let no corrupt communication proceed out of your mouth, but that which is good to the use of edifying, that it may minister grace unto the hearers."*

Are we exempt from acting upon this verse when we are facing these physical hardships? Could we stand before God, using them as an excuse, and say something like, "Now God, I know your Word says that I am not supposed to speak words that are harmful. When I speak to people, my words should build them up, encourage them and strengthen them. My words should bestow favor and blessing upon their lives. But God, when I said those mean things to my (spouse, friend, child, or whoever), I couldn't help it. I was mad. And besides, I was excused from acting upon your Word because of my physical condition."

Do you think God is going to change His Word because our bodies are changing, or the pain is intense, or we didn't get enough sleep?

Please don't take me wrong. I am not down-playing the reality nor the seriousness of these physical conditions. But I am encouraging you to let God's Word answer these questions for you. Don't allow your natural human reasoning to lead you. Proverbs 14:12 and 16:25 say:

> **There is a way that seems right unto a man, but the end thereof are the ways of death.**

We cannot lean to our own understanding if we truly want to be set free.

Right and Wrong Thinking

There is something else we need to consider before we start blaming our emotions, attitudes or actions on our physical conditions.

Have you, or someone you've known, ever had an argument with someone, and the further it went the madder you got, to the point that you lost control of your temper? Then, with your emotions unchecked and your voice raised, you spoke mean and hurtful things. And then, all of a sudden, right in the middle of your rage and fury, someone entered the room. It may have been a friend, a parent, a child, your Pastor, your boss, or someone you didn't even know. So, you immediately gained your composure and acted like nothing was wrong. You may have even conversed with the third party for the next few minutes, speaking to them and treating them with kindness. Then, after they left the room, you unleashed your rage and fury once again.

There are probably a lot of people that will read this and say, "Yes, that has happened to me." Then let me ask you a question. Why did you change the way you were acting when someone entered the room?

You might say, "Well, I didn't want them to know we were fighting," or "I didn't want them to think badly about us." Why didn't you want them to know? Why were you concerned about what they would think? Maybe it was because you would have been embarrassed. Maybe the person who walked in was someone you didn't want to disappoint, or someone that could have an effect on your future. Whatever the reason for your change in actions, *you changed!*

Someone may say, "Well, Brother Larry, I was just *acting* like everything was okay."

Listen, if someone is acting, then there is action involved. So, we may say that we are just acting calm or acting like nothing is wrong, but the fact is *we are still changing our actions.*

Now remember, the whole premise of what we are discussing is that we *"can't help the way we are acting"* because of some physical condition. But the above illustration shows us that we *can* help the way we are acting, no matter what is going on inside our bodies.

Okay, now let me ask you this. What was it that made you change your actions in the above illustration? Someone may say, "It was the person that entered the room." But guess what? That is not true. It wasn't the person that entered the room that changed your actions. That person, no matter who they were, could not make you act a certain way.

"Well then, Brother Larry, what was it that made me change the way I acted?"

Your thought pattern changed. You see, what you were thinking before they entered the room was different than what you started thinking once they came in. And when you thought something different, you changed your actions.

The truth is, you were not putting on an act at all! You were just acting like your normal self. You were acting just like you always had around them in the past, when everything was going well. But, when your *thoughts* changed, your *actions* changed!

Do you know what the word *acting* means? It has been defined as *the art or practice of representing someone or something*. In other words, acting is when we act like someone or something.

Now let me ask you another question. When that person entered the room, how did you start *acting*? I would guess that you were kind, gentle, lovely, peaceful and maybe even smiling, as though you had some joy in your heart.

You might say, "Well, yes—but remember I was just acting!" Okay, let's look again at the definition of acting. It is when you *act like or represent someone else.* So—when you were acting kind, gentle, lovely, peaceful and even joyful—who were you acting like? I would venture to say that you were *acting like a Christian. You were acting like Jesus!*

The Bible says in Ephesians 5:1 for us to imitate, or act like, God. The previous verse tells us to be kind, tenderhearted and forgiving toward one another.

James 1:22 tells us to be doers of the Word. That means we act upon God's Word whether we feel like it or not. The 2nd verse of James tells us to *"count it all joy"* when we are faced with troubles and difficulties. That means we are supposed to act like we're full of joy, regardless of what is going on around us or inside our bodies.

I could go on and on, but the point I want to make is this: *when you chose to act nice and act like everything was okay, you were controlling your emotions.* You actually took control over your feelings and actions. In fact, you were acting in a normal manner. On the other hand, when you were yelling, sowing strife, being unkind, etc. you were acting in an abnormal way.

It may have been a fact that you were experiencing a physical condition in your body when you unleashed your emotions. However, since you were able to control yourself in the presence of the second person, then you could have controlled yourself around the first one—*if you had chosen to!*

In reality, it wasn't your hormones, the medication, or the pain that made you act a certain way. If that were true, then you would have continued to yell, be unkind, etc., even when the second person entered the room. However, when he or she entered the room, you thought something different, and that changed the way you acted.

What you were thinking determined your actions.

Proverbs 23:7 says, *"As a man thinks in his heart, so is he."* In other words, whatever we are thinking about will ultimately control our actions.

Here is something else we must consider: The physical conditions that we are discussing are not part of the inward man. In other words, they are not a part of you. You are a spirit being, you have a soul and you live in a body. These physical challenges are something transpiring inside the body, not inside the spirit.

So, I'm going to ask once again, can we exercise authority and dominion over our bodies even when all of these things that we discussed are going on inside of them? Is it possible that God's Word will work for us regardless of what is taking place inside of us or outside of us? Could it be that Smith Wigglesworth did have a revelation that would benefit all of us? Maybe we do have more dominion and authority in this natural realm than we realize.

CHAPTER

10

Dominion Over All

Look at Genesis 1:28.

> **And God blessed them** ["them" means
> male and female], **and God said unto
> them, Be fruitful, and multiply, and
> replenish the earth, and subdue it: and
> have dominion over the fish of the
> sea, and over the fowl of the air, and
> over every living thing that moves
> upon the earth.**

God told both the man and the woman, *"have dominion...over every living thing that moves on the earth."* Notice, He said we have dominion over *"every living thing."* Every living thing would include bears, sharks, snakes, dogs, spiders, etc., but what about living things in our bodies? Are our organs living things? Are infections, viruses and diseases living things? Are our cells, muscles and brains living things, even when they are being affected by physical exhaustion or medication?

Whatever it is that is affecting our bodies, it is living, and God said we have dominion over EVERY living thing. Did He mean it? I believe He did. Therefore, whether it's a *"grizzly bear"* moving on the ground, or a *"grizzly hormone"* ☺ moving in our body—we have dominion over it!

"But Brother Larry, didn't Adam lose that dominion when he sinned?" Yes—but Jesus (the Last Adam) redeemed us and gave us back the dominion that the first Adam lost. In fact, Ephesians 1:19-23 says we have authority over all *"principality, power, might, dominion and every name that is named."* Well, is hormone a name? Is pain a name? Then can exercise authority over them. This is a truth that we must take hold of—we have dominion and authority over our bodies.

Look at 1st Corinthians 9:24-27.

> **Know ye not that they which run in a race run all, but one receives the prize? So run, that you may obtain. [25]And every man that strives for the mastery is temperate in all things. Now they do it to obtain a corruptible crown; but we an incorruptible. [26]I therefore so run, not as uncertainly; so fight I, not as one that beats the air: [27]But I keep under my body, and bring it into subjection: lest that by any means, when I have preached to others, I myself should be a castaway.**

Verse 24 lets us know that our life here on the earth is likened to a race, and that God wants us to win the race! Verse 25 tells us that as we strive to win, we must be temperate or self-controlled. It also shows us that an incorruptible crown is waiting for us at the finish line. Verse 26 tells us that we are not running aimlessly or fighting without purpose.

Now here's the interesting part. Verse 27 tells us that we must keep our bodies (not our spirits) under complete control or we will end up as losers, disqualified from the race!

Let's take a closer look at what the Holy Ghost said through the Apostle Paul. He said, *"I keep under my body and <u>bring it into subjection</u>."* He calls his body an *"it."* To further our understanding of what he is saying, let's look at some other translations.

"But [like a boxer] I buffet my body [handle it roughly, discipline it by hardships] and <u>subdue it</u>."
(The Amplified Bible)

"I harden my body with blows and <u>bring it under complete control</u>." (The Good News Translation)

"I beat my body and <u>make it my slave</u>." (NIV)

"I buffet my body, and <u>lead it captive</u>."
(1890 Darby Bible)

"I discipline my body like an athlete, <u>training it to do what it should</u>." (The New Living Translation)

I underlined what we are supposed to do with regard to our bodies. Notice, we are supposed to *"bring it into subjection... subdue it... bring it under complete control... make it our slave... lead it captive... and train it so it will obey."*

Who is supposed to do those things?

Paul said *"I"* do this to *"my body."* He distinguishes the body from the inner man. So the inner man is the real you. And you have dominion and authority over the outer man, the body.

In Romans 12:1 and 1st Corinthians 6:20 we are told to present our bodies to God as a living sacrifice and also to glorify God in our bodies. Those verses don't say that God is going to do something with our bodies. They say that we have to. Why do you think God tells us to do something with our bodies? Because He has given us dominion and authority over our bodies and now He expects us to control them. Well, if we have dominion over our bodies, then we have dominion over every part of our bodies—including our hormones!

Listen ladies, when your hormones start stirring up a storm on the inside of you, you need to follow Jesus' example and say, *"Peace, be still!"* Then boldly confess what God says about your mind and emotions.

This will keep your eyes fixed upon God's Word. Matthew 6:22 says, *"The light of the body is the eye: if therefore your eye is single, your whole body shall be full of light."* I like the way The Living Bible states it: *"If your eye is pure, there will be sunshine in your soul."*

Take hold of this truth. It will change your life. You—the spirit man on the inside—can control the way you feel. Don't let your body control the way you feel. In fact, here is some truth that will really bless you. Look at Galatians 5:22 again. When this verse lists the fruit of the Spirit, it starts with *"love"* and ends with *"temperance."* The Greek word for *temperance* means *self-control.* Yes, you did read it right—it means SELF-CONTROL!

God has given us the power and ability to walk in love, have His joy, experience His peace...and (at the end of the list) exercise total control over ourselves! Wow! Because God's Spirit is on the inside of us, we can control ourselves—totally! WE can control our spirits, our minds, our emotions, our bodies, our finances and anything else that belongs to us. Glory to God! You should be getting very excited by now because your future is looking brighter!

CHAPTER

Partaking of the Divine Nature

Allow me to strengthen your faith some more by looking at 1st Peter 1:2-4.

> **Grace and peace be multiplied to you through the knowledge of God, and of Jesus our Lord, ³According as his divine power has given to us all things that pertain unto life and godliness, through the knowledge of him that has called us to glory and virtue.**

⁴Whereby are given unto us exceeding great and precious promises: that by these you might be partakers of the divine nature, having escaped the corruption that is in the world through lust.

Did you notice in verse 2 that grace and peace can be multiplied to you? Well listen, when we are facing physical challenges in our bodies, that is the time when we need grace and peace multiplied! God's grace is sufficient for us to overcome every hardship, and His peace will keep us emotionally stable right through them.

So, how do we get the multiplication factor to work during our physical challenges? We are told in verse 2, it is *"through the knowledge of God and of Jesus."* Verse 3 tells us that God's divine power has given us *"all things"* that pertain to our lives. And, once again, they are obtained through the knowledge of Him. Verse 4 tells us that the knowledge of Him will give us *"exceeding great and precious promises"* and that we can use these wonderful promises to *"partake of His divine nature."*

Wow! Did you hear that? We can partake of the very nature of our Father God! I wonder if He ever flies off the handle, feels like quitting, throws a pity party or decides not to love us anymore? Of course not!

Then we don't have to allow those feeling to control us either! No matter what our bodies are going through, God's Word is still true and it works. And, according to God, it works for whosoever, any and all! If you fall into one of those categories, then you qualify! Therefore, since God said that we can partake of His nature—we can! And He didn't say that His divine nature is not available during times in our lives when our bodies are going through changes or experiencing pain.

Now remember, I am not belittling what you or anyone else is going through, especially a woman who is facing menstrual disturbances or one who is going through menopause. Obviously, I am a man and don't have to deal with the same chemical and biological issues that women do. It is virtually impossible for me to understand or feel the way a woman does. However, one thing is for sure, GOD AND JESUS UNDERSTAND IT ALL!

The Scripture reveals that God is *Omniscient*. Omniscient is a word that means *knowing everything*. Scripture declares that God's eyes run everywhere, and He searches all hearts and observes everyone's ways. In other words, *He has complete knowledge about everything and everybody at all times!* So don't you think He understands your hormones and your feelings? Of course He does. And don't you think that He has made a way for women to overcome those things in their bodies, even when those things are trying to influence their emotions? Of course He has. Look at what He said in 1st Corinthians 10:13 from The New Living Translation.

> **But remember that the temptations that come into your life are no different from what others experience. And God is faithful. He will keep the temptation from becoming so strong that you can't stand up against it. When you are tempted, he will show you a way out so that you will not give in to it.**

Listen, all of us, both men and women, are going to face life's pressures. They will tempt us to act in a way that is contrary to the way the Bible tells us to act. But God has made a way of escape for every single person—male and female!

If you will go back through this book, you'll find out that God didn't exclude men or women who were going through the changes of life, from experiencing His peace and joy on a continual basis.

For example, we looked at Galatians 5:22. Notice God didn't say, "The fruit of the spirit is love, joy, and peace—unless you are a man going through your mid-life crisis."

We also looked at Romans 8:6. Notice God didn't say, "To be spiritually minded is life and peace, unless you are a woman going through menopause."

> *God didn't exclude anyone, at any time,*
> *from enjoying His divine nature*
> *on a continual, uninterrupted*
> *and never-ending basis!*

Isn't that good news? Yes and Amen!

Let me say it again, WE HAVE DOMINION OVER OUR BODIES. But we can't dominate our bodies without the Word of God. Turn over to James 3:1, and let me show you something else in this regard.

If any man offend not in word, the same is a perfect man, and able also to bridle the whole body.

Look at what the Amplified Bible says, *"And if anyone does not offend in speech [never says the wrong things], he is a fully developed character and a perfect man, able to control his whole body and to curb his entire nature."* In other words, if we don't say the wrong things, we can control our whole body, and restrain (or keep in check) our entire nature. So, if we fill our heart with God's Word and keep it full, then our mouths will speak out of that abundance, and release life-filled words that control the whole body—which includes our hormones! Glory! However, if we just say what our bodies say, and what the doctors say, and what human nature says, then we will not be able to rule our bodies and bring them into subjection.

In this same chapter of James, we are told that we shouldn't have blessings and curses coming out of our mouths. In other words, when we are feeling good we talk kindly, but when we are feeling bad we speak unkind words. James tells us that this kind of action should not be taking place in our lives.

Proverbs 18:21 tells us that our tongues can release life-filled words, or words that are filled with darkness and despair.

Joshua 1:8 tells us that if we will speak God's Words, meditate upon them continually, and act upon them, then we will prosper and be successful in everything we do.

Proverbs 6:2 tells us that when we guard our tongue, we will be in charge of our lives.

Proverbs 18:7 says, *"A fool's mouth is his destruction, and his lips are the snare of his soul."*

Proverbs 21:23 informs us that when we guard our mouth and tongue, we keep ourselves from trouble.

The list goes on and on. So let me ask you this: Do you think God would tell us to guard our words if we couldn't control them? I don't think so. Therefore we have the means to control our emotions no matter what is going on inside OR outside our bodies.

Now remember, our words are controlled by our thoughts. So, if we allow ourselves to get mad, and display ugly emotions in front of some people but not in front of others, then during those times of emotional disorder we are choosing the wrong thoughts. However, God has equipped us and given us the ability to think positive, helpful, and lovely thoughts all the time, and to bring captive the ones that are not godly.

Proverbs 4:23 says, *"Keep your heart with all diligence; for out of it are the issues of life."*

The Good News Translation says it this way: *"Be careful how you think; your life is shaped by your thoughts."* The New Century Version says, *"Be careful what you think, because your thoughts run your life."*

Simply put, WHAT YOU THINK IS GOING TO CONTROL WHAT YOU SAY AND DO (i.e. YOUR ACTIONS).

So, what do we need to do so that we think and speak the right things, and so that our bodies do not control our emotions? Well, since Proverbs and James both tell us to control what we say, let's glean from their wisdom.

Proverbs 4:23 tells us to guard our thoughts, but the previous three verses tell us how. They tell us to *pay attention and make a continual effort to hear God's Words, to never lose sight of His Words, and to keep our hearts full of them.*

James 1:25 calls God's Word *"the perfect law of liberty."* And it tells us that if we want to be happy and blessed, *we must fix our eyes upon God's Word and always keep it in view.* We must keep looking at it, no matter what is going on inside of us or outside of us. That is, *we must persevere, remain faithful, and be committed to seeing what it says, and then applying it to our lives.*

We must act like the Word is true no matter how we feel, and regardless of the actions of others!

At this point I will remind you of a verse that we already studied in this book. Philippians 4:8 tells us to *think upon things that are true, honest, just, pure, lovely, of a good report, virtuous and praiseworthy.*

The only way we can continually think these kinds of thoughts is to continually hear and speak what God's Word says. In fact, this is how we *"cast"* our cares upon the Lord. Remember 1st Peter 5:7? The Greek word for *casting* means *to throw off.* The same word is used in Luke 19:35 when it says, *"they cast their garments upon the colt."* That means there is action involved.

So, what is the action that we must take in order to *cast our cares?* Well, how did those cares come to us in the first place? They came through our minds, in the form of thoughts. Therefore, when we don't take those thoughts, but rather replace them with God's thoughts (through our words and meditations), that causes the wrong thoughts to be cast away and keeps us living carefree!

If we will make the choice to do what the previous verses in James, Proverbs and Philippians tell us to do, it will bring us into a life that is full of peace and joy. And it will take us far from a life that is filled with worry and stress.

Making that choice will enable us to control what we think, what we say, and how we act, even during those times when we are in pain, on medication, tired, or going through hormonal changes.

Wow! This revelation is truly life changing!

CONCLUSION

Faith Brings Victory

I'm going to close this book by going to one final passage of Scripture. We have already seen that Jesus overcame every obstacle in this world for us so that we could experience a restful and serene life. He left us His supernatural peace and joy so that we could maintain control of our emotions. So the question becomes, "How do we bring this kind of life into reality? How do we walk it out day by day? How do we exercise this supernatural peace and overcome all life's difficulties?"

Look at 1st John 5:4.

For whatsoever [whosoever] *is born of God overcomes the world: and this is the victory that overcomes the world, even our faith.*

Let me quote this verse from two other Bibles. The Good News Translation says: *"Every child of God is able to defeat the world. And we win the victory over the world by means of our faith."* The Message Bible reads: *"Every God-begotten person conquers the world's ways. The conquering power that brings the world to its knees is our faith."*

The means to achieve victory over fear, stress, worry, anger, unforgiveness, depression, etc. is *our faith.* Our faith in God's peace and presence will cause us to conquer the world's ways. Our faith in God's Word and God's ways will release His power into our lives and bring the world to its knees. And, I might add, *our faith can bring our bodies to their knees as well!*

Faith is not something that is hard to understand. It just means simple, child-like trust. Let me give you an example. When I was about 3-4 years old, my family moved from the city to the country. We moved onto property that bordered a spring-fed lake. My dad built a dock out over the water. One day I was standing on the dock and my dad was standing down below in about five feet of water. He said to me, "Come on, Larry, jump! I'll catch you."

Now what do you suppose I did? Do you think that I stood there and thought, "What if I jump and he's not telling the truth?" or, "What if I jump and he misses me? I'll surely drown."

No, I didn't think those things. As far as I was concerned my daddy couldn't lie, and since he said that he would catch me then I knew he would! And so I leaped off that dock with only my daddy's word to rely upon. I couldn't go by past experience—I didn't have any. I couldn't go by other people's experiences—it didn't matter, this was MY daddy. I had complete trust, or faith, in him and his word.

That is all God is asking of us—simple child-like trust. Since we are born of God, then He is our Father and we are His kids. We are in the world but not of the world. We are to reign in this life by the strength of the Greater One who indwells us. We have His Name, His Blood and His Word.

Now let's go overcome—*by the blood of the Lamb and the word of our testimony!* (Revelation 12:11)

I Have Finished This Book—Now What?

For further feeding, more revelation and increased strength we offer three other resources. Our tape series, *"Heavyweight Champion of the World"* will help you to gain more understanding about using your faith to overcome the problems of life. Our Scripture tape *"Power Up"* will empower you on a daily basis to live victoriously. It is daily bread that is full of faith, victory and power, and will give you the energy and strength that you need to be a winner every day. And then we strongly recommend our Scripture tapes *"Wisdom Scriptures."* It has been said that a proverb a day will keep the doctor away. Well, I don't know about that, but I do know that God said, *"Wisdom is the principal thing; therefore get wisdom.* (Proverbs 4:7) *"Wisdom Scriptures"* is our 4-tape collection of the entire book of Proverbs. It will fill your life with wisdom and open the doorway for all of God's blessings to come into your life. All of our Scripture tapes (which have no preaching, just Scriptures being quoted from multiple translations over a musical background) come in either CD or cassette, and are available through our website at: www.lhm.net .

Finally, ***reread this book***. Your faith will grow, your understanding will increase and your ability to overcome every obstacle of life will surge forward in a mighty way!

VERY IMPORTANT MESSAGE

God wants a personal relationship with every person in the world, including you! God is not mad at you, and He is not counting up all of your sins and holding them against you. He sent Jesus Christ to shed His blood, die on the cross and then be raised from the dead. And He did all that just so that you can be freed from the bondage of sin and enter into eternal life with a loving Heavenly Father.

If you have never accepted Jesus Christ as your personal Lord and Savior, it is very simple to do. The Bible states in Romans 10:13, *"Whosoever calls on the name of the Lord shall be saved."* Since it says, *"Whosoever"* then your name is in the Bible! Verses 9 and 10 tell us how easy it is to receive salvation (eternal life). They tell us that if we will say with our mouths that Jesus is our Lord, and believe in our hearts that God raised Him from the dead, we *"shall be saved."* It is that easy!

If you have never accepted Jesus as your Lord and Savior, then do it today! Say the following prayer out loud—right now:

Dear God, I want to be part of your family. You said in your Holy Word that if I would acknowledge that you raised Jesus from the dead, and that I accept Him as my personal Lord and Savior, I would be saved. So God, I now say that I believe you raised Jesus from the dead and that He is alive and well. I accept Him now as my personal Lord and Savior. I accept my salvation from all sin right now. I am now saved. Jesus is my Lord and Savior. Thank you, God, for forgiving me, saving me and giving me eternal life. Amen!

If you just prayed this prayer for the first time, I welcome you to the family of God! According to the Bible, in John 3:3-6, you are now born again. Now it is very important, as a newborn child of God, that you get fed the milk of God's Word so that you can grow up in God and become a mature Christian.

If you will take the time to write, fax or e-mail us at the addresses listed on the contact information page, we would love to send you some free literature to help you in your new walk with the Lord. We will also be more than happy to help you find a good church that preaches the Word of God—not the traditions of men. This is vitally important for your future success in God.

Finally, come see us sometime. We would love to meet you! Our itinerary is included in our free magazine *The Force of Faith,* as well as on our website.

God Bless You!

Dr. Larry J. Hutton

Other Materials
From
Force of Faith Publications

<u>Books</u>

➤ God, the Gold, and the Glory:
        Glorifying God through Personal Increase

<u>Teaching Tapes - Series</u>

➤ The Goodness of God
➤ Healing School
➤ Jesus the Healer
➤ Healing Made Easy
➤ How to Change Your Circumstances
➤ The Rich Young Ruler:
        The Story You've Never Heard
➤ Final Countdown:
        Your Launching Pad to Financial Freedom
➤ Heavyweight Champion of the World:
        Overcoming the Problems of Life
➤ Roof Rippin' Power:
        Activating God's Power for the Miraculous

Teaching Tapes - Singles

- Faith to be Healed (How to Keep Your Healing)
- No More Blue Mondays
- God's Healing Medicine
- Questions and Answers on Healing
- Redeemed From Sickness
- Don't Quit: Your Miracle is Here!
- Working for a Living: It's a Trap!

Scripture Tapes and CDs

- Heaven's Health Food:
  Healing and Health Scriptures
- Heaven's Wealth Food:
  Prosperity and Wealth Scriptures
- Power Up:
  Victorious Living Scriptures
- Wisdom Scriptures:
  All of Proverbs (a 4-volume set)

Music Tapes and CDs

- The Greatest Gift (Larry's Singing Album)
- Peace Be Still (Instrumental: Piano & Strings)
- Perfect Peace (Instrumental: Piano only)

To Contact
Larry Hutton Ministries
Write:

Larry Hutton Ministries
P.O. Box 822
Broken Arrow, OK 74013-0822

Or use one of the following methods:

Phone: (918) 259-3077
Fax: (918) 259-3158
E-mail: admin@lhm.net
Website: www.lhm.net

*Please include your prayer requests
and comments when you contact us.*

ABOUT THE AUTHOR

Dr. LARRY J. HUTTON is a dynamic teacher and preacher for the body of Christ today! He teaches and preaches with a prophetic voice that is changing the lives of multitudes.

In 1980, God spoke to Larry in an audible voice and said, "Keep it simple, my Word is simple!" With that mandate from heaven, Larry has become widely acclaimed for the clarity and simplicity with which he teaches God's Word. He believes that the Bible is for us today, and that we ought to be able to understand what it is saying so we can apply it and reach our God-given potential. He also believes that we don't have to wait until we get to the "sweet by and by" to enjoy God's blessings. Larry emphasizes that God wants us to enjoy His blessings in the "sweet here and now!" Through plain and practical teaching, Larry shows us what those blessings are, as well as how to receive and enjoy them.

Larry is nationally and internationally known as a speaker, TV host, author, singer and songwriter. He has become a popular guest speaker at church meetings, seminars, campmeetings and on Christian television. His teachings about divine healing, prosperity and victorious Christian living have challenged and helped many ministers and laymen alike around the world to strive for God's best in their lives.

While his ministry produces a wide variety of audio and video teaching aids, Larry is perhaps best known for his unique and extremely popular series of Scripture tapes, "Heaven's Health Food," "Heaven's Wealth Food," "Power Up" and "Wisdom Scriptures." Available on CD or tape, they feature Larry speaking multiple translations of many verses applicable to the title subject, thereby bringing incredible clarity to the Word. Presented over a soft instrumental background, these unique products lend themselves to repeated listening. As a result, thousands of people have been healed, encouraged and set free by "hearing and hearing" the Word of God as presented on these tapes and CDs.

LARRY HUTTON MINISTRIES also publishes and distributes a free magazine called *The Force of Faith*. Read by tens of thousands of people, its articles are educational, uplifting, inspiring and encouraging.

Larry, his wife, Liz, and their daughter, Rachel, travel extensively, and conduct regularly scheduled meetings at the LARRY HUTTON MINISTRIES headquarters in Broken Arrow, OK.

Additional copies of this book are available from
LARRY HUTTON MINISTRIES, INC.

FORCE OF FAITH PUBLICATIONS
Broken Arrow, OK 74012